1104 BROAD STREET

a memoir

Mary Rocap

Me from the Somethyme years; photo by Jonathon Moss, 1974

Mary Rocap

singer and songwriter, author, quilter, baker, star gazer, and chronicler of her backyard flock of chickens

Also by Mary

BOOKS

LITTLE CHICKEN STORIES

MORE LITTLE CHICKEN STORIES

SAVING TIME: A FABLE

FAITH & ARTS: A RETROSPECTIVE: 2010-2020

RECORDINGS

SWEET MIMOSA

INDIAN SUMMER

DEEP DECEMBER DREAMS

SPRING: THE WIND'S STORY

HALLELUJAH! AMEN.

WWW.MARYROCAP.COM

ISBM: 978-1-387-83253-8

COVER ART BY STEVEN RAY MILLER

1104 BROAD STREET

a memoir

Mary Rocap

Me from the Seventh Street years; photo by Tom Prince, 1986

Timeline of Ownership

SOMETHYME

July 1973 - August 1975: Elmer Hall, Mary Rocap, Mary Bacon

September 1975 - March 1976: Elmer Hall, Mary Rocap, Mary Bacon, Martha Maiden

March 1976 - December 1976: Mary Rocap, Mary Bacon, Martha Maiden

January 1977 - December 1978: Mary Bacon, Martha Maiden

December 1978 - June 1983: Mary Bacon

June 1983 - November 1984: Mary Bacon, Mary Rocap

November 1984 - December 1985: Mary Bacon, Mary Rocap, Jenny Wears

SEVENTH STREET

January 1986 - June 1986: Mary Rocap, Jenny Wears, Lise Uyanik Ebel

June 1986 - December 1986: Mary Rocap, Jenny Wears, Lise Uyanik Ebel, Jill Cotter

early 1987 - March 1988: Mary Rocap, Jill Cotter (active owners)

March 1988 - June 1993: Jill Cotter

The Restaurant Family Tree

Somethyme: October 17, 1973 - December 31, 1985

Pyewacket: May 17, 1977 - May 2002

Anotherthyme: May 1, 1982 - October 2009

Seventh Street: January 1, 1986 - June 1993

My Chart

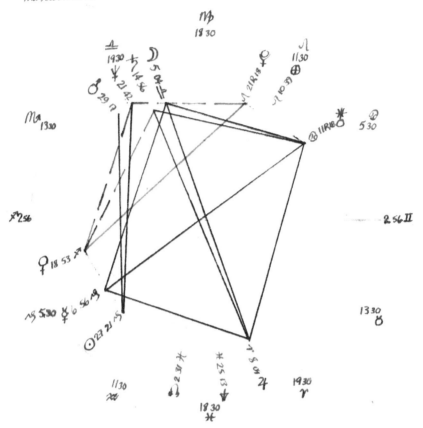

Mary Recap
4 a.m., E.S.T.
18 January 1952
Brynmawr, Penn

E 2   C 8
A 4   m 2   ♎ ♈
F 4   F 1
W 1

masculine (8·3)

3 ♂ "two men playing chess."
the transcendent ritualization of conflict; objectification.

Chart prepared and drawn by Martha Maiden

Somethyme's Chart

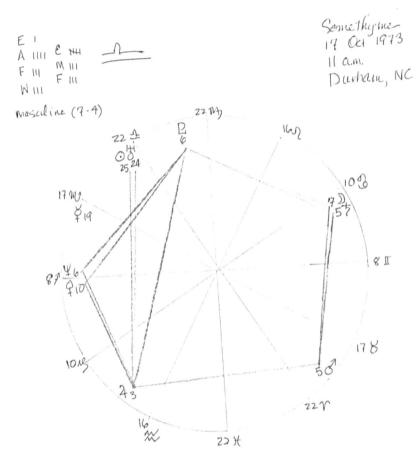

E I
A IIII   C ++++
F III   M III
W III   F III

masculine (7·4)

Somethyme
17 Oct 1973
11 a.m.
Durham, NC

8♐ "Rocks and things forming therein"
learning how to awaken hidden energies

Chart prepared and drawn by Martha Maiden

The Meaning of Our Names &
Our Astrological Signs

ELMER: noble, famous
Taurus

MARY: bitter, rebellious, beloved
Mary Bacon: Cancer
Me: Capricorn

MARTHA: mistress (feminine of the "master")
Scorpio

JENNY: lady of the people, gracious, merciful
Aries

LISE: God's promise
Virgo

JILL: youthful, a child of God
Aries

Introduction

In 1973, fresh out of college, I, along with two people I barely knew, opened a restaurant. It was one of those things, maybe lucky, maybe not, that happens when you are young and brave or when you don't know any better: a quick decision, not fully vetted, that ends up casting a long shadow. At the very least, the restaurant became a lodestone keeping me tethered for eighteen years. And perhaps, even now, its draw is not diminished as I have spent several years writing about it. I have written mostly for myself, but also with the thought that others might be interested in the tale.

In starting to put pen to paper, I realized I needed more than just my memories if I was to give a good accounting, because my memories are getting shorter all the time. So I started to look around for actual documents. Fortunately, I am a saver of things. I have old menus, a scrapbook album full of restaurant memorabilia, and a three-ring binder with two years' worth of kitchen meeting notes. I've got journals, calendars, letters I wrote my mother, and letters she wrote to me.

As I pored over all of this material, I began to notice that things I have been telling myself over the years might not, actually, be the truth – not wholesale lies – but slanted, or slightly out of whack, versions of the story. So, right off the bat, I feel it necessary to state, I have to accept that I am not who I think I am. I've always told myself that I am a Steady Person. Trustworthy. Dependable. In reading my entries about the restaurant, I am totally phasing in and out. I go from being a full-time owner, to part-time-owner, to shift worker, to manager, back to owner, then shift worker, and finally just the bookkeeper. I am in, wanting to be out; I am out, wanting to be in. I don't seem to be able to work things through, and so I leave, and then I come back to try all over again. Was there any growth? Maybe, maybe not. Some of the issues at the beginning were still there at the end. Did I gain wisdom or did the story just get longer?

Also, I know that memories are unreliable and it's hard to tell the whole story when there are pieces that remain missing or hidden. And frankly, I have preferred, in some cases, not to dig too deeply, lest I waken unbidden ghosts. That said, these pages recount eighteen years of my life given over to the service of the restaurants Somethyme and Seventh Street. Those years brought both bitterness and joy. This writing may be an act of trying to reconcile the two. It's not meant to be a tell-all, a getting my-side-of-the-story out, a big reveal, a getting even. It is a story I tell to myself, and now to you, and I tell it with fondness and tenderness, with a full measure of love. Everyone who was there saw it, lived it, and tells it according to their own experience. This is mine.

Somethyme

OCTOBER 17, 1973

1104 BROAD STREET, DURHAM, NORTH CAROLINA

Those are the markers, the when, the where. We're coming on a half century and I still inhabit that place, or rather that place still inhabits me. Somethyme intrudes into my dreams, arises in my thoughts, connects my present to my past. Somethyme Restaurant was formative in making me who I am. I believe I hold that in common with anyone who worked there, especially in the early years. It occupied a time and place when time and place and food and art and politics and community, above all community, mattered. We all worked there doing the daily making and serving of food, knowing that the work was symbolic of so much more. Was it ideal? No. Was it fraught? Yes. In many ways I never understood the arc of our existence: the in-the-moment magical beginning, the toiling middle, and the everything-unraveling end. Our world was 20-some tables and a stove top with six eyes – it held and holds an expansive and enduring significance far beyond what its dimensions would suggest.

Bev Dawson setting up the front; photo by Jonathan Moss, October 1974

The Stove; photo by Jonathan Moss, October 1974

The restaurant was housed in a nondescript storefront on an unimposing stretch of Durham, North Carolina, three blocks north of the stone wall surrounding Duke University's East Campus. Swift Avenue dissects the meandering road connecting the two campuses: East and West. It changes its name to Broad once it crosses Main Street and then goes on and on into the hinterlands of Durham County. Somethyme sat on the boundaries of three neighborhoods: Watts Hospital/Hillandale, Old West Durham, and Walltown.

Watts Hospital/Hillandale was known for its stately tree-lined Club Boulevard. Willow oaks which were planted in the 1920s, became a leafy canopy which provided luxurious shade and allowed the street to live up to its name. Residences set back from the road were picture perfect – each one with its own unique design. While it was not the grandest of Durham's offerings it exuded class. It was established in the early 1900s when Watts Hospital was built. Watts, now the site of the public residential NC School of Science and Math, was a private hospital funded entirely by the manufacturer, banker, and philanthropist George Washington Watts. The hospital operated from 1909 to 1976 serving Durham's citizens, unless you were Black. It was a middle- to upper-class white neighborhood.

The second neighborhood of note was Old West Durham. This is the one the restaurant faced. Its history predated Durham and had originally been known as Pinhook. A pinhooker was someone who made cigarettes and cigars from poor quality tobacco that had not sold at auctions. Pinhook began as a "traveler's rest" with lodging and places to eat that attracted hardscrabblers who were a bit on the rough side. Once the Erwin Cotton Mill was built in the 1850s, the area was settled by lower-class white mill workers who lived in houses the mill provided.

Walltown, just behind the restaurant, was named after George Wall. Born enslaved, he purchased a lot in 1906 and built a home for his family. The surrounding area gradually became a residential neighborhood of African Americans employed by Duke University in service and construction jobs. While Club Boulevard also bounded Walltown, no willow oaks had been planted along its sidewalks. By the 1970s, the neighborhood had lost much of its proud heritage and was transitioning from Black folks who lived in their own homes to a bi-racial neighborhood of renters. Because of its proximity to Duke and the cheap rents, the neighborhood swelled with students and former students. This led to the gentrification that exists there today, side by side, with efforts to reclaim its political and historical roots.

All this is to say that 1104 Broad Street was not unlike the center of the universe, the waystation from here to there: equal measure city, university, and neighborhood; East and West; white and Black; rich and poor; working class and professional.

•~•

Duke University, for all its perceived and maybe intended separateness, had a complicated and intertwined relationship with the city. Because Somethyme would not have existed were it not for Duke, we shared that same knotty identity. The restaurant was situated in Durham and we owners did live within city limits, but the locals did not consider Somethyme a home-grown business. The founders, Elmer Hall, Mary Bacon and I, all called Durham home only because of our individual connections to the university. And yet, Somethyme rose to become a Durham institution despite our alien transplanted cultural roots. Durham would come to claim us as its own.

I want to describe Durham as I came to know it as a student at Duke. In the early 1970s, Durham was classified as a small city having a population of around 100,000 (one third of its size today). Although Duke tried to offer everything a student might need on campus, there would be things that only Durham could provide (including a hefty dose of reality).

To the east of Duke's walled-in East Campus lay "Five Points," the edge of Durham's downtown district. I, like many Duke students, became familiar with the topography of the city: its businesses, eateries, and churches; its red-brick factories and county-seat courthouse. For a Duke student, city life was just a short walk away. The bus station on the far side of downtown was the jumping-off place to anywhere: whether that was an out-of-state connection via Raleigh's train station or simply a bus ride over to Chapel Hill's Franklin Street for more interesting shopping than what the local Northgate Mall could offer. If you weren't a Methodist wanting to worship at Duke Chapel, there were churches and a synagogue within several blocks of the campus. Sears had a large store downtown, where I bought my first bike. There were women's and men's fancy clothing stores, shoe shops, drugstores, furniture stores, lawyers' offices, banks, travel agencies, a library, a hardware store, a jail, and a hotel. The mammoth Book Exchange would buy your last semester's books and also housed library-sized stacks of used books for purchase. And Morgan Imports, with its colorful displays of quirky items, was the first shop you came to as you began your stroll downtown.

A fire had gutted the downtown district in 1914, so much of the rebuilt commercial area has a consistent appearance. The buildings are sturdy, well-made, and built-to-last structures made of brick and stone with stylish accents, be it Art Deco or Neo-Classical. At the time, Durham also had a distinctive smell: the sweet and heavy scent of cured tobacco, especially noticeable once you hit Gregson Street. The city had been built on the back of tobacco following the Civil War and there were block-long cigarette factories on either side of Main Street where you would be given a pack of Lucky Strikes if you took a tour. The downtown area had not yet been decimated by suburban malls, but a cloud of uncertainty hovered above the business community. The fact that, (misleadingly named) Urban Renewal had razed the Black business district on Pettigrew Street and adjacent Black neighborhood, Hayti, in order to create the Durham Freeway added to the unsettled atmosphere. All told, the homes of some four thousand families and the locations of five hundred businesses were destroyed. At that time, Durham was about 61% white and 39% Black. Today, both percentages are lower: it is 45% white and 37% Black reflecting an increase in the populations of Hispanic (13%) and Asian (5%) peoples.

The Durham Bulls, a minor league baseball team, which is so much a part of Durham's identity today, was inactive between 1972 and 1979. The team had been founded in the early 1900s. They began playing again in 1980 at the baseball field made famous by the 1987 movie *Bull Durham* starring Kevin Costner, Susan Sarandon, and Tim Robbins. Durham built the team a new stadium in 1995. Our claim to fame connecting the restaurant and the movie was that Susan Sarandon ate at Seventh Street during its filming.

• ~ •

Somethyme was on the north side of Duke's East Campus. Although I never recall walking that far down Broad Street as a student, it was within walking distance. The 1100 block of Broad Street between Englewood Avenue and Club Boulevard was strictly commercial and attracted local patronage rather than business from the university. On our side of the block was an auto parts store (Reilly's), a florist (HK Sanders), a music equipment store (John Troy's Soundhaus), a frame shop (House of Frames), a laundromat (Norge Village), a drug store (Revco) flanked by two parking lots, and a bank (Central Carolina Bank). All the businesses from the laundromat to the florist were packed together cheek by jowl, but each had a distinctiveness that set the one apart from the other. The opposite side of the street had a gas station (Melton's), a funeral home (Clements) and a bar & grill that served burgers, hot dogs and delicious French fries (The Top Hat). There were other businesses that are not etched into my memory other than Beautiful Day Natural Food Store which opened a few years after Somethyme, closing once Wellspring Grocery opened around the corner on Ninth Street. The laundromat, bank, and drug store were very helpful to have as neighbors, and we utilized their services heavily.

These businesses were owned or run by locals. With our ties to Duke, we were seen as a bit of the odd man out (or even worse – odd woman out), greeted with a "You're not from around here, are ya" sentiment. Over time, we settled in comfortably with our neighbors with the possible exception of Clements who kept their distance and never warmed up to us, nor us to them, to be fair.

1104 Broad Street had been built in the 1940s and was owned by Ralph and Inez Keaton. The basement had originally been an auto repair shop with wide doors opening into service bays. The street level space was outfitted as a restaurant. 1104 was a long and lean red brick building with a flat roof and floor to ceiling windows which faced the street. Those windows were a conduit, a portal, a looking glass from one world into another. Our "different-ness" was on full display. In time it would be obvious to anyone driving down Broad Street that something was happening here: the line of long-haired young people wearing tie-dyed clothes interspersed with conservatively dressed older women with permanents and clutch bags waiting to get in was a dead giveaway.

Somethyme (Open Durham photo)

A Map of Durham:

THE RESTAURANT, VARIOUS PLACES I HAVE LIVED, AND THE PLACES MENTIONED IN THIS WRITING

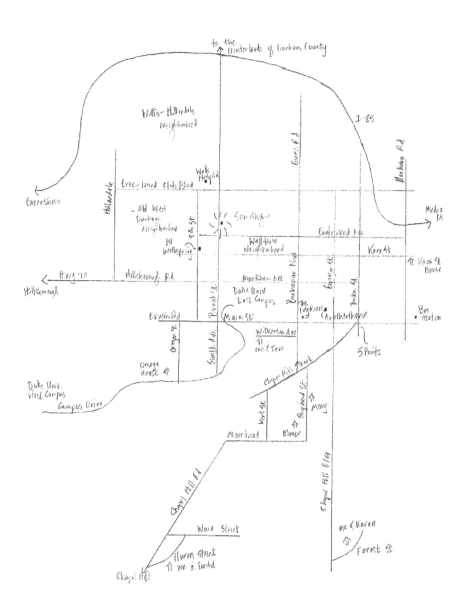

Before the Beginning

All stories have a beginning. When it is your life, though, just how far back do you go?

I'll start with my arrival at Duke University as a college freshman in the fall of 1969. I came from Media, Pennsylvania, the county seat of Delaware County, which boasted a trolley down its main street and its own train station on the line going back and forth from Philadelphia's 30th Street Station. We lived just three blocks from the center of our small town and my father, an attorney, walked to his office. Our backyard bordered an undeveloped patch of woods leading down to the train tracks. I probably spent more time in the woods and backyard than on the streets of town.

My father had gone to Duke, both for his undergraduate degree prior to WWII and then to law school, following the war. He was a Duke-forever fan. I have memories of the school from childhood because he brought us down south, as a family, to visit in 1959. Maybe the fact that he was so keen on Duke made me disinclined to consider it, so I applied to other schools: Grove City, Albright and, because I loved New England scenery, the universities of both New Hampshire and Vermont. Also, I knew Duke was a good school, a hard-to-get-into school, and I didn't think they'd accept me if I was to apply not being an exceptional student: an A minus to solid B. For some reason, my math teacher, Mrs. Elliott, suggested I look at Duke. This has always surprised me as I reflect back over my life. Her gentle nudge catapulted me into what my life would come to be. With her encouragement I broached the subject with my parents. My father was overjoyed and immediately called a fraternity brother he had kept in touch with who worked in admissions. Despite the fact that the application period had already ended, his friend assured him they would take my application. Surprisingly, they accepted me. Once accepted, there was no longer a question of where I would go to school. Now I know this to have been a Legacy Acceptance. My younger brother also went to Duke, but he got in on his own considerable merit.

My first day on campus; photo by my mother, Ann Rocap, September 1969

I arrived with Villager outfits, a pixie haircut, a guitar, folk music albums (The Brothers Four, Odetta, Judy Collins), wall posters, and an accent that identified me as a northerner. By the time I went home at Christmas, I was wearing bell-bottomed blue jeans with frayed hems and had already begun to fall in love with the sound of the Carolina cadence, the slower spoken and gentler voiced southern drawl.

In 1969, all the dormitories for women were on East Campus. Unlike the men, we had a curfew; we were not allowed to live off campus.

Nobody had cars. By the time I graduated in 1973 all that had changed. The Vietnam War changed that. Nixon, Race Relations, Societal Class Relations, Worker's Rights, Women's Rights changed that. The spring of 1969, the academic year before I arrived, was noted for the "Allen Building Take-Over," a protest launched in support of African American students' demands which included the creation of an African American Studies Department and the accessibility of more financial aid for Black students. This was a big deal and I always felt I had missed something important in the Duke identity that my upper classmate friends had forged.

The Kent State Massacre on May 4, 1970, in which four unarmed students were killed and nine others injured by the Ohio National Guard occurred in my freshman year. Those killings were both unimaginable in horror and eminently imaginable to a student body also engaged in peaceful protest against the Vietnam War on campus. To quell the potential for violence, the administration suspended all classes, cancelled exams, and adopted a simple pass/fail grading system for the semester. This action enabled the student body the time, space, and freedom to respond to the Massacre. I, along with friends, signed up to do neighborhood canvassing. We were sent out in teams of two to talk to Durhamites about becoming more informed about what was going on in the country and, in particular, the injustice and immorality of the Vietnam War. The people in the neighborhood to whom we were assigned answered our knocks and listened courteously, but nobody invited us in.

From that time on, the politics of protest took hold and there was no let-up of marches, "teach-ins" with invited speakers, and vigils, both on and off campus. These activities birthed a whole new model of "higher" learning. As a consequence, more of my education came from what was happening outside the classroom than from within. I was not an activist or a rabble rouser by any stretch of the imagination, but

I was concerned enough to show up to meetings and lectures and in 1971 to caravan up to the March in Washington with friends. But, I must admit, politics and protests aside, I was very relieved to receive a pass rather than an actual grade in my classes that freshman year.

The times demanded engagement and I recognized that. What one might do professionally following graduation was given less consideration than what one should do in the world right now to create a better place and become better people – more ethical, more engaged, more neighbor-loving, more political, more intentional. That kind of energy was there from 1968 to the mid-70s, leading many Duke students to put down roots, prioritize community, claim Durham as their home, and change it some in the process.

As a freshman, I was assigned to Alspaugh Dorm and lived there my first two years along with about 120 other women. As a rising junior, I applied for membership in a one-year experiment of living within the framework of an intentional community sponsored by the Methodist Campus Ministry. This co-ed community, Omega House, was on Oregon Street, midway between the two campuses. The previous year's Omega House was, possibly, the first co-ed living arrangement sanctioned by Duke. The Methodist Campus Ministry building had been repurposed into suitable housing for residents. It had a chapel (with nice acoustics for playing my guitar), a large commercial kitchen, and lots of offices that became bedrooms for the twelve who lived there. Because there were more of us than could be accommodated, a second location was secured on Knox Street as a satellite Omega House. The house on Knox Street, in the Old North Durham neighborhood, was within biking distance to the campus. At the time, Durham had zoning regulations which disallowed more than two people unrelated by blood or marriage to rent a house together. They had to apply to the City Council for a zoning waiver in order to sign the rental agreement.

There were a variety of advisors who met with us weekly, on a rotating basis, including: campus minister Milton Carothers; religion professor The Rev. Dr. Robert Osborn; history professor Dr. William Chafe; zoology professor Dr. Peter Klopfer; and weaver Silvia Heyden. Their role was to lead a house course on the history of utopian communities: their failures and successes and how those might illuminate our own experience of communal living.

I'm not sure how many of these intentional living experiments there were. I know there was the one prior to ours and at least one after. And, whether or not the experiment was a success is debatable. What the proof of its success would have been I don't know, but I enjoyed the experience much more than that of living in the dorm. I always felt like I was a stranger in Alspaugh; those in Omega House felt like fellow travelers. There was a camaraderie amongst us even though we weren't all cut from the same cloth. Our ranks included a football player (the only member of the team not recruited) and an artist; religion majors and science majors; and a spread of ages ranging from two graduate students to two sophomores. I felt at home in a way I never had during my freshman and sophomore years. I liked the off-campus dynamic. I wasn't surrounded by architecture that reminded me of my status as a student. I was learning about who I was. I liked the emphasis on gathering for meals and enjoyed the associated chores: cooking, setting up, and cleaning up. We never fully bonded, but we were all honing our values. Some of us did end up becoming an on-going community, and that group has remained in close contact all these years hence. Others from Omega House I have lost track of.

The summer after my "experimental" junior year, I moved into the Knox Street house "for real" with others from Omega House, officially became a Durham citizen, and never looked back. But by then, I was already well on my way to adopting Durham as my hometown. When walking or biking is your primary mode of travel, you can't help but come to know a place. The details of the path become intimate, they begin to become a part of your life's outer and inner landscape. In addition to my treks downtown, I had come to know its neighborhoods by walking to fellow students' houses who lived off campus. Durham is a patchwork of neighborhoods with great names such as Trinity Park, Morehead Hills, Braggtown, and Monkey Bottom. The neighborhoods had personalities as their names suggest. Those early years helped foster a connection that still informs my sense of belonging. When I drive the streets of Durham today, half of my mind is paying attention to what I'm doing while the other half is wandering down memory lane, remembering who lived where, way back when.

The Knox Street house was in a quiet established neighborhood. We adopted "Knox Street" as our "family" name; individually, we were Knox Streeters. We had a dog, "Happy Hotdog." a little dachshund. We never called ourselves a commune; we were more like a household. We were definitely not just a bunch of people renting rooms in the same house. We ate together, shared the housekeeping, shopping, cooking. We hung out together and had house meetings to sort things out when necessary. It was there that I began to bake bread.

I began to bake because I missed the homemade bread I had grown up with. My mother baked weekly, usually on Thursdays, when my great-grandmother, Fiddy, would come for the day. Fiddy had been born in 1865; she died at 98 when I was eleven. Now when I think back on how many years the combination of our two lives touched – us holding hands in the middle – history of, say the Civil War, doesn't seem so long ago – it's within my imagination's reach. Mom used Fiddy's bread bucket. These days a bread bucket is more of an antique item than a common household fixture so I will describe it: It's a three-gallon metal bucket about a foot high with a crank attached to the lip of the bucket, a lid that slips under and around the crank, and a clamp that holds the whole thing onto the table it sits on. The bucket comes with handy instructions embossed onto the lid: "Put in all liquids first then flour / turn 3 minutes / cover . . ." As the instructions instruct, you put all the ingredients into the bucket, you knead the dough by turning the crank, and the dough rises within the bucket. You don't remove the dough until it is time for it to be shaped for its second rise in the bread pans. Fiddy's bucket was a Universal Bread Maker #4, a 1904 model. I don't remember being taught to bake, I don't remember turning the crank. I only remember pinching off pieces of dough and hiding in the closet to eat the contraband. Since I didn't have a bread bucket at my disposal at Knox Street I made do without. With *The Tassajara Bread Book* as my guide and recipe book, I launched myself into baking. The bread bucket is now in my possession, but it sits on a shelf. I continue making bread using the bowl, whisk, and paddle technique that I learned at Knox Street. I keep the bucket on display as a testament to my roots.

One bread lesson I learned was that, left unattended, bread dough can sour. I remember starting a batch of oatmeal-rye and then someone coming by and suggesting an activity out of the house. It was either something I was keen on doing or someone I was keen on doing something with, but without too much thought, I left my dough with the notion that I could just finish it later. Well, when I did come back, it was deflated and smelled terrible. I had to throw the whole thing out and start over another day. That was a lesson I never learned from my mother – she always finished what she started.

I and another Knox Streeter both took part-time jobs at Kentucky Fried Chicken – a short walk down Roxboro Road from the house. I worked there during my senior year and was still working there following graduation. I had double majored in history and religion, and Milton Carothers tried to interest me in a job at one of the big churches in Chapel Hill on Franklin Street doing "women's ministry." I did not want work at KFC forever, but I just could not see myself in such a role, plus I didn't feel I was "grown-up" enough to hold a "professional" position like that.

I don't know who told me that Elmer Hall was thinking about opening up a restaurant. As the chaplain at Duke and advisor to the YM/WCA, he had a high profile amongst people I knew, although I had never met him personally. Born in Gibsonville, North Carolina, not overly far from Durham, he had attended High Point College, transferred to Northwestern University in Chicago, and after college served in Singapore with the Peace Corp. He returned to the states and went to Duke for his graduate work in religious studies and became an ordained Methodist minister with a Buddhist bent. He had been serving as chaplain for six years. He was active in anti-war and radical politics. In many ways he was unorthodox, opening up his home to other like-minded folks, including undergraduate students, and was living in community with them.

Regardless of who told me, I biked over to his house on Shepherd Street on Wednesday, June 20, 1973 to talk to him about my baking bread for him should he open a restaurant. Despite his radical reputation, when he opened the door I found him to have a gentle demeanor, sparkly and crinkly eyes when he laughed, and an easy way about him. My calendar notates this as "Bluebird Talk." Bluebird was the name of a hippie vegetarian restaurant which had recently closed. I'm fuzzy on the details, but I walked out of his house knowing that, at the very least, I could be on the staff as a baker or that, shockingly, I could join him as a full partner in the enterprise. This was exciting to me. I was definitely on board for being the baker and not put off by the offer of partnership. It was, in fact, something I could imagine myself doing: baking bread, preparing food, and being part of a working community.

• ~ •

But let's step back a bit and consider the obvious: by any conventional marker, how was I even a prospective partner candidate? One, I was young. Two, I was inexperienced. While I considered myself a baker, and loved to bake, I had never baked in quantity or for hire. Three, I was not a restaurant aficionado. Before the restaurant opened, I was not in the habit of going out to eat, in no small measure due to a lack of expendable cash. And four, no one would ever describe me as a foodie. I didn't have a passion for food – not even a slight bent towards food. I was not an adventurous eater. I was a cautious, suspicious-of-food eater. Mom would call me a picky eater. I am still a picky eater. As a child I didn't eat a host of foods including mushrooms, olives, blue cheese, oysters, sauerkraut, and most vegetables, but especially not lima beans. As an adult, I have improved in the vegetable category, now eating brussel sprouts, turnips, collards, black beans and kidney beans, and (late to the party) okra.

My upbringing was in a home- and church-centered setting in the 1950s and 60s. I was the oldest of three; Mom was a full-time homemaker. She made most of the clothes that she, my sister, and I wore, and she prepared all the family meals. Dinner was always ready at 5:30. Daddy and we children were responsible for washing, drying, and putting away the dinner dishes. We ate as a family and always said grace. Although I remember Spam, Rice-A-Roni, TV dinners, and Tang, in general Mom baked and made things from scratch. Meals weren't fancy, unless it was your birthday. If it was your birthday you got to pick your meal, even if Mom had never made it before. Like duck. Like Baked Alaska. She didn't stock soda in the fridge and, as my parents did not drink alcohol, there was never any wine, beer, or liquor in the house.

Seldom did we go out for dinner. Every once in a blue moon, Daddy would take us to Howard Johnson's, where I would always get fried clams and then mint-chocolate chip ice cream for dessert. Aside from eating at a drug store counter, I cannot recall a single other restaurant we ever went to, as I was growing up, either regularly or irregularly.

The exception to this was when we were on vacation. Despite being economically conservative most of the time, as our standard camping vacations would imply, there was a sense of self-indulgent freedom when we were on these month-long road trips. A case in point: On a trip to the New York World's Fair in 1964 when I was twelve, we began overhearing raves about something called a Brussels Waffle. So we queued up in the long line at the Belgian Village. Once seated and served, we were all properly impressed, jaw-droppingly impressed, at the majesty of this dish. The waffles were light and deeply crevassed; the strawberries were red, ripe, and juicy; and the whipped cream was bountiful. It was maybe the most delicious treat we had ever had, certainly one of the most beautiful.

In Canada we often enjoyed fish and chips wrapped in newspaper from street vendors. At that time cod was plentiful. All the fishing villages had carefully constructed cone-shaped piles of salted cod drying out in the open. There were also privately owned outdoor bread ovens in abundance. On the Gaspe Peninsula we stopped at a house displaying a sign for fresh bread and upon receiving the still-warm fragrant round loaf, immediately and unceremoniously, began to tear into it. Since this was in stark contrast to our usual table manners, we gave this style of eating a name. From then on, we would call this "hunking it." We returned the next day for another loaf, an extravagant use of gas. Another memory is stopping at a house with the sign "fresh fish." The man who lived there told us to wait a bit so he could check his line. He came back with a fish which he then fileted for us. We decided that his fish was as fresh as fresh could be.

The other food influence from my growing-up years that comes to mind is that my parents had a ministry of hospitality for foreign students studying in the US. In particular, there was a large group of Indians who gathered at our house for monthly dinners. From these dinners, I learned to make pooris (a circle of unleavened dough rolled thin and then fried, causing the dough to entirely puff out), and I fell in love with their way of cooking rice. I would decline the spicy sauce and just fill up on "Indian Rice." Later at the restaurant, Apura Islam would make his version of this rice, Polaw, when we had our international dinners. I have his recipe, written out in his own hand, and refer to it when I make it now. It calls for basmati or jasmine rice (washed then roasted), onions caramelized in butter, fresh ginger, cinnamon sticks, whole cloves and cardamom pods, salt, rose water, saffron, and boiled raisins.

The background I came from was one of stretching pennies and eating plain nutritious food. Mom made sure there was fresh bread on the table at every meal and something for dessert after dinner. She had a three-cookie-limit rule (but cookies were much smaller back then). When I was a young mother, my girls had a two-cookie limit. Nowadays, cookies have gotten so big, it would have to be a half cookie.

I should also add that once we children left the nest, my parents became the foodies they probably always wanted to be, subscribing to

Gourmet and *Bon Appetit* and enjoying eating at the best restaurants Philadelphia and New York City had to offer. I still consider myself foremost a bread baker, but I became a bit of a foodie as well, although I continue to avoid mushrooms, olives, blue cheese, oysters, sauerkraut, but above all, lima beans.

• ~ •

Fortunately Elmer did not consider my inexperience and lack of knowledge a handicap perhaps because, philosophically, we were aligned. As a household, Knox Street was part of the get-back-to-the-land, you-are-what-you-eat generation. We were early members of The People's Intergalactic Food Conspiracy Co-op, a brazenly named co-op that still exists, although no longer using that name. All co-op members worked shifts assembling orders and other such tasks. We ordered and received fresh eggs, whole grains, organic staples and perishables. We bought a tiller and planted a house garden. Our meals began to be more likely vegetarian than meat based. It was Political as well as Social. Environmental as well as Ethical. It was Cuisine with an Attitude. Elmer must have seen something of that in me.

Intrigued by our conversation and his idea of a restaurant, the following day, Thursday, June 21, Elmer and I met at the site, 1104 Broad Street, to look the place over. We returned on Friday for what I called "Bluebird Clean-Up." And then, on Monday, June 25, we met at The Ivy Room Restaurant and talked formally. The Ivy Room would become a favorite spot to meet for restaurant planning. Since the very next day I was leaving for Pennsylvania to join my folks on a month-long camping trip to Alaska, I didn't commit to being his partner, but I did give him a strong "maybe" with the proviso I needed to think about it a bit. Reflecting back, that was a big ask and a big risk on Elmer's part. I am so grateful that he took a chance on me. On the camping trip, I decided it *was* what I wanted to do. I called him from a pay phone in Fireside, British Columbia, milepost 543 of the Alaska

Highway, to say "Count me in."

It was at this point Elmer alerted me that there was a complication. While I was away, he found that someone else was also looking at the Bluebird spot to open a restaurant: Mary Bacon. Although Mary had grown up nearby, she and her husband, David, were newly returned from California. David had been stationed there while serving in the Navy and was now enrolled in Duke's Forestry Graduate Program; Mary was working at the Durham County Mental Health Center.

Elmer had talked with her and thought we might have compatible visions but wanted me to meet her before going forward. When I got back in early August, we all met at The Ivy Room and talked about our plans. Elmer's were that he wanted to create a place for the community, serving wholesome, healthy, vegetarian (plus fish) food in a place which actively tried to walk the walk: politically, socially, ecologically, and spiritually. It was to be the embodiment of his beliefs that he had been espousing in his capacity as Duke Chaplain calling for social change, peace, non-violence, and non-racist practices. At first glance, Mary struck me as emotive and affectionate with a sharp eye compensated for by a ready smile. It was clear that she was passionate about food and eager to begin work. She had been dreaming of opening a restaurant and cooking full-time; she had developed lots of recipes and was sure that she could come up with a killer menu. I'm not sure what kind of vision I offered, but I must have tried to create a compelling image: I was in a short-lived period of smoking cherry cigars and I lit one up. What I knew was I wanted to do work that was consistent or in harmony with my fledgling identity and that this particular work, this restaurant, felt right to me. I was ready to give it my all which, admittedly, wasn't that much, other than a love for baking and a willingness to work hard.

Elmer and Mary in attendance at my first wedding; photo by Martha Maiden,
June 8, 1975

POST SCRIPT: It turns out that it was Tom Campbell who told me about Elmer starting a restaurant. Tom emailed me after reading an early copy of the book saying he told me about Elmer and told Elmer about me. Thank you for that, Tom!! Tom was a friend of mine and of Knox Street and knew I was a baker. He would go on to co-found Regulator Bookshop on Ninth Street – a business that became another of Durham's cultural hubs.

The Partnership

All in all, I'd have to call us an unlikely trio. Lately, I had the thought that Elmer supplied the *"Why"* of the endeavor: he was the restaurant's visionary. Mary was the *"What"*: she brought the fabulous food; and I might have been the *"How:"* a worker bee with an eye for work flow and a knack for keeping disparate people and threads together. We were completely unknown to one another: we were a happenstance collision of orbits. Had it not been for Somethyme we probably would not have sought each other out; our paths might never have crossed. Yet, regardless of the many unknowns, we pledged to give each other the benefit of the doubt. We cast our lots together and moved forward. It turned out there was a balance, a harmony in the blend.

In 1973, only 5% of businesses were owned by women; in 2022 the percentage is over 40%. Although our partnership was not 100% female when we began, it was decidedly mostly-female. I don't remember discussing this prior to our opening: that women-owned businesses were few and far between. I never got the impression that Elmer considered Mary and me to be second-best partners because we were women. Nor did it feel like some kind of glass ceiling to Mary and me. In retrospect, it must have been very clear to Elmer that going into business with two women was contrary to the prevailing custom. Of course, Elmer was a bit of the contrarian. He was also a man of the cloth and his understanding of God and seeing God in all persons may have led to his ease of partnering up with not just one, but two Marys.

Besides the unconventional feminine slant of our partnership, there was a decided age differential. Elmer was 16 years older than me: 37 to my 21; Mary was 27. I felt that difference keenly. Mary seemed so much more experienced than I and Elmer was almost in another generation. In 1973, no one in my circle of friends owned the house in which they were living, but Elmer did. It was an elegant one with real furniture. A house in line with his position at Duke. At the time, he was planting some kind of evergreen tree that would grow fast and straight and provide a natural fence on his side yard. This was well beyond the kind of make-do-with-what-you-had world that I lived in. I wondered how he had come to have that kind of knowledge: knowing what to plant. And, Mary was already married. None of my friends were married yet. Plus, she had such great sense of style and decor. Every room in her house had artwork on the walls, colorful pillows on the couches, and candles on the tables. Both Elmer and Mary exhibited a level of sophistication that I had yet to acquire.

Even going into it, I knew for a fact that the restaurant would not happen without them. They could do it without me, but I couldn't do it without them. I didn't have the dream, the ambition, or the confidence. As a result, I couldn't help but be ambivalent about my role in creating it. The words "My Restaurant" did not roll off my tongue; it was "The Restaurant" that I was most comfortable with. So, despite being fully committed, engaged, and proud to be part of the undertaking, taking ownership of the ownership was never easy.

Coupled with my ambivalence was the fact that they were much more comfortable being in the spotlight. The two of them would become far more front and center from the outside looking in, even from the inside looking out. I was not the mouth piece. I was not the face. You could always find me working away in the back, behind the scenes, and off to the side.

But in spite of the unconventional nature of our partnership, from that initial blind trust came so much that was good, even with the hard times we would come to endure. Principally for me, beyond the creation of the restaurant itself, Somethyme is where I would meet my second husband, Tom Prince. It is where Charlie Ebel, Lise Uyanik, and I would begin a long and fulfilling journey of performance and song; where my association with Georgann Eubanks and by extension, Donna Campbell, would come to enrich my creative life in ways I could not have imagined; where deep and lasting friendships were forged, some of which have continued into the second generation; and it is where I learned skills that I would use in subsequent work settings. There was a goodness to the Mary-Elmer-Mary (MEM) partnership that continues to this day.

The Days of Preparation

If not Providence, then the Timing was surely favorable. It was 1973: a time of can-do, a time when it did not cost an arm or a leg to try something. Were this to happen today, it would be impossible. The money needed has changed considerably. The expectations of customers have risen as well. Not to mention the tightening up of building codes. We started with a combined investment of $13,000 and a low threshold need of income. I could make ends meet with $25 a week.

By the time that meeting at The Ivy Room concluded, we resolved that we could and would come together as equal partners. We began working together in earnest. We were on our way to something unknown, but were completely unfazed. We were in the moment and buoyed by the so-called horizon of a "change is gonna come," the "dawning of the Age of Aquarius" if you will. You could feel it. We all could. If you had been there you would have felt it too.

Our predecessor, the Bluebird Café, had been owned by Nona McKee. It was the first vegetarian restaurant in Durham. Somethyme is often given that designation, but that is not accurate. Nona was a good cook with a quirkiness about her that was endearing. From our perspective, the closing of her restaurant, in May 1973, looked unplanned. It looked like one night she had had enough and just walked out, locking the door and throwing away the key. A couple months later, food from that night, was still out. Rotten and smelly. What was inside the now-unrefrigerated walk-in cooler was infested with maggots and roaches.

Her boyfriend, Billy Stevens, negotiated on her behalf, and on August 14, we bought the entire contents of the place: tables, kitchen equipment, and the unbelievable mess. Nona was always welcome at Somethyme and often would visit and chat, especially in the mornings.

We struggled with a name for the place, finally settling on Manifestation or Manna Fest Station. We liked its many layers of meaning. Taken all together, manifestation bespoke of an underlying truth made visible. Teasing out the parts you get:

- Manna: God's provision of bread for the Israelites hungry and lost in the desert, or "grain of heaven, the bread of angels" as the psalmist describes it (Psalm 78);
- Fest: a gathering, a festival, a feast, a festivity; and
- Station: a place.

Close to our opening, an interview with Elmer was published in the September 28, 1973 edition of the Duke campus newspaper, *The Chronicle*. In it he said: "I've been serving bread and wine to students since 1967, I'm just broadening my menu." I love that quote. Manna Fest Station was a tidy way to describe Elmer's ecclesiastical vision. It is also evidence that, from the outset, the restaurant had a depth to it that once opened was never adequately developed. It was something Elmer brought to the table and his leaving took that dimension with him.

We did agree that it was a mouthful, but we also thought people would call us The Station as a nickname. However, as it turned out, Manna Fest Station would not be our name. A friend of a friend suggested the name "Somethyme" to a Knox Streeter. We all liked it straight away. It had a certain airiness to it, both beautiful and graceful, that to this day retains its charm. Even though we were within weeks of opening and were already using bank checks printed with Manna Fest Station, we changed course. So glad for that!! In a letter to my folks dated

September 24, 1973, I wrote: *p.s. We changed the name to "Somethyme."*

In the body of the letter I wrote:

"The Station is taking up most of my time 7 days/week – all hours. I am tired and feel tense a lot – not enough time to myself or with [Knox Street]. Elmer, Mary, & I are getting along fine considering the amount of time we are spending together. Most of the time I feel good but I have lapses of insecurity and feel incompetent, but I am sure everything will work out fine. The building is being transformed now and that is very exciting. It will be beautiful. Just ordered $90 worth of spices which freaked me out. Will spend $1,500 just on food – isn't that incredible?"

Preparing the place took a lot of work, but we had a lot of help. Loads of folks pitched in: Knox Streeters, friends of Elmer's, Mary's sisters, and even my out-of-state sister, Carol. Architect friends supplied the front design and carpenter friends built it. Many more supplied grunge labor to clean the place up and do other non-skilled tasks. We installed dropped ceiling tiles over portions of the front seating area. This broke up the long rectangular space and helped define different areas which gave the place an intimacy and interest that it had not had before. We stripped the old wallpaper from the walls, painted them, and then hung beautiful woven African tapestries semi-permanently loaned us.

We bought a tobacco barn from a Mr. Herndon and went to his property in Chatham County, which seemed so far away at the time, to pull down its weathered wood siding and remove its smooth thick round supporting posts. We nailed the siding to the right wall creating a façade, used it to build the bar and cashier stations, and had enough left over to construct a narrow back hallway, shielding the bathrooms. That barn wood lent a warm and inviting feel and the posts held up the dropped ceiling.

Looking at the bar and towards the back; photo by Ann Rocap, 1984

Duke Chapel had recently suffered an interior fire and Elmer used his connections to get a couple pews no longer needed which we installed as seating in the back section. He also got some lovely sconces for the walls. I actually still have one of those.

The kitchen was in the rear and featured windows all along the back wall which gave a wonderful feeling of expanse and light to the workspace. There was a walk-in cooler, a hood and exhaust system, a six-burner gas stove with a flat top griddle and broiler, a steam table, a short-order refrigerator unit, and an air conditioner we called the "swamp cooler." We washed the dishes manually using the three-sink method: the first sink for washing; the middle sink for rinsing; and the last sink, with its electric coils heating the water up to 180 degrees, for sterilizing. There was a second set of sinks for pots and pans. Pretty much everything else in the restaurant was built by hand: front tables and booths, kitchen work tables and shelves, pantries, wait stations, the bar, the cashier station, the kitchen mezzanine.

What the building lacked was a back door. What commercial building does not have a back door? Surely this was a safety and fire department regulation issue. This was also a trash removal issue. The city would not allow us to put our trash out on the curb, forcing us to rent a dumpster and place it behind us in the back alley. But how to get our trash into it? There was a decided slope from the front of the building to the back which made taking the trash out cumbersome. The solution was nifty but would forever cost us points on the rating we got from the health department's inspection. We removed a kitchen window section and built a trash chute that led to the dumpster below from the opening above. We tossed every bag of trash and garbage down that chute with a big heave-ho.

We would also get points deducted for having no designated hand sink and using so much wood in the kitchen (prep tables and shelving) instead of the favored stainless steel. The best we could ever do was a 93 grade: still an A, but a dangerously low one.

We wanted everything to be beautiful and distinctly ours. We painted the kitchen avocado green, a color fairly representative of that era (actually, the 1973 pantone color of the year) and were horrified when the health department informed us that we would have to paint over it. Nothing but regulation white would do.

Over time, many others added to the beauty and efficiency of the place:

- Richard & Lonna Harkrader were the designers of the seating area and loaned us the tapestries;

- Rachel Preston made the decorative macramé piece that initially hung in the doorway and she planted and maintained a flower garden out in the front;

- Russell Rigsbee made stained glass inserts for the door, a stained glass hanging lamp, and at least one table (we paid him a bottomless cup of coffee which he took full advantage of);

Looking towards the front; photo by Ann Rocap, 1984

- Bev Dawson made countless aprons and table cloths;

- Larry and Sue Anderson (Anders Hill Pottery) made large indoor planters for the ledge between the booths as well as the cream pitchers and sugar bowls using their distinctive mottled teal glaze;

- Robin Moran made so many things there is no way to list them; she was our go-to carpenter and built what we needed;

- Dave Birkhead, Bruce Blevins, cyn croxton, Linda Huff,

Rochelle Kalish Hunt, Marilyn Roaf, and Sue Sneddon designed and/or contributed artwork to our menus;

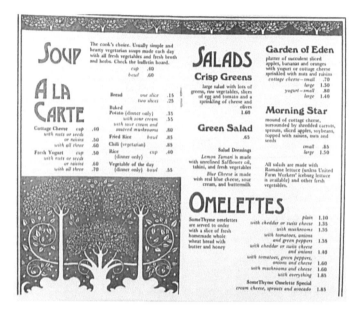

This Dave Birkhead's menu design was my favorite

Marilyn Roaf's whimsical summer menu

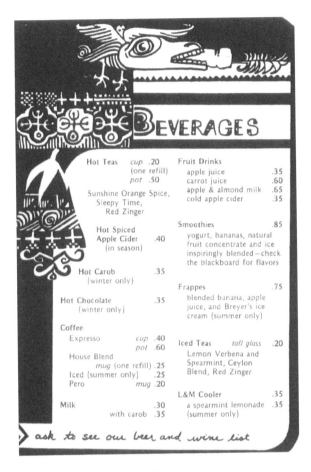

Hot Teas *cup* .20
(one refill)
pot .50

Sunshine Orange Spice,
Sleepy Time,
Red Zinger

Hot Spiced
Apple Cider .40
(in season)

Hot Carob .35
(winter only)

Hot Chocolate .35
(winter only)

Coffee
Expresso *cup* .40
pot .60
House Blend
mug (one refill) .25
Iced (summer only) .25
Pero *mug* .20

Milk .30
with carob .35

Fruit Drinks
apple juice .35
carrot juice .60
apple & almond milk .65
cold apple cider .35

Smoothies .85
yogurt, bananas, natural
fruit concentrate and ice
inspiringly blended — check
the blackboard for flavors

Frappes .75
blended banana, apple
juice, and Breyer's ice
cream (summer only)

Iced Teas *tall glass* .20
Lemon Verbena and
Spearmint, Ceylon
Blend, Red Zinger

L&M Cooler .35
a spearmint lemonade .35
(summer only)

ask to see our beer and wine list

cyn croxton's artwork on a beverage menu

- Celeste Wesson created our logo: our name with the spice jar, onion, and pepper;

- Geb Adams recreated Edward Hopper's "Early Sunday Morning" on the wall of the men's bathroom; and

Wicca Paull graced the women's bathroom with a painting of her own.

We took a lot of pride in the appearance of the restaurant. I remember the smile of satisfaction on the faces of our esteemed clean-up crew, Nancy Wharton and Jeff Marterer, after taking all of a Monday to wash, strip, wax, and buff the checkboard-patterned front linoleum floor. In a way, in hindsight, this amazes me. We were, most of us, children. I hardly knew enough to keep my own room clean. But we applied ourselves to the task at hand, whatever that task might be. We learned new skills. We committed ourselves to showing up day after day to make food and serve it in a place we had created that was beautiful to our eyes.

. ~ .

POST SCRIPT ONE: Mr. Herndon, it turned out, was not happy with what we removed from his tobacco barn. In particular, he declared he had not given us permission to take those posts out, as I found out years later. Tom and I went into his second-hand shop, which he called his "warehouse," with, count 'em, 26 cats. Its entrance was at the top of a steep set of stairs to the second floor. You could find anything and everything there. He recognized me (or I may have reminded him of who I was) and then proceeded to give me quite a talking to – saying that he would be in touch with a lawyer – that he intended to sue us. Although his words were alarming, he never followed through with his threat. I never went back.

POST SCRIPT TWO: Here is a really odd or funny thing: in 2017, a skinny little shop with the address of 1104 ½ Broad Street opened with the name of Manifest Skate Shop. It specializes in skateboard supplies. It is as if the name, Manna Fest Station, was bound and determined to be used in the 1100 block of Broad Street. It just had to wait until the time was right.

Let's Remember:
What was going on in 1973?

NATIONALLY:

- Abortion was legalized in the landmark decision Roe vs. Wade by the United States Supreme Court;
- Members of the American Indian Movement occupied Wounded Knee, South Dakota for 71 days;
- Secretariat won the Triple Crown;
- The Watergate Hearings began and President Richard Nixon declared, "I am not a crook;"
- Vice President Agnew resigned;
- The Endangered Species Act of 1973 was passed to "protect species and the ecosystems upon which they depend;"
- Skylab, the United States' first space station, was launched;
- Billie Jean King beat Bobby Riggs in "The Battle of the Sexes" exhibition tennis match;
- The Inflation Rate was 6.16%;
- The Unemployment Rate was 4.9%; and
- Minimum Wage was $1.60.

INTERNATIONALLY:

- The Paris Peace Accords was signed on January 27, 1973, ending the U.S. involvement in the Vietnam War;
- The Yom Kippur War began and the Oil Embargo caused the price of oil to increase by 200%;
- Basque Terrorists killed the Spanish Prime Minister;
- General Augusto Pinochet led a military coup in Chile;
- Israel shot down a Libyan passenger plane;
- The Irish Republican Army bombed King's Cross Railway Station, London; and

- The Concorde cut the flying time across the Atlantic in half, flying at an average speed of 954 miles per hour.

We Watched a Bunch of Movies:
- The Exorcist
- Deliverance
- Live and Let Die
- Last Tango in Paris
- Jesus Christ Superstar
- American Graffiti
- Lady Sings the Blues
- The Sting

Words that Entered Our Vocabulary:
- Black Hole: a hypothetical hole in outer space into which energy and stars and other heavenly matter collapse and disappear;
- Body Language: the unconscious gestures of the body as a form of communication;
- Bummer (slang): a bad experience;
- Ecocide: the destruction of the suitability of the earth's environment for living things;
- Jane Crow: discrimination against women;
- Knee-Jerk: reacting in a predicable or automatic manner;
- Male Chauvinism: excessive male pride or exaggerated loyalty to members of the male sex;
- Ms: abbreviated title used instead of Miss or Mrs.;
- Participatory Democracy: active participation in the public arena to achieve some right or to protest an injustice;
- Power Structure: the institutions and groups that make up or control a society, especially as they determine the character or nature of a society;

- Street People: a term for hippies or others who have rejected traditional social values including homes, so that they are usually found congregating on streets, in parks, and other public places; and
- Zero Population Growth: the condition in which a population ceases to grow and a balance is reached in the average number of births and deaths.

WOW, LOOK AT THESE PRICES:
- The average cost of a house was $32,500;
- The average annual income was $12,900;
- The average monthly rent was $175;
- The cost of a gallon of gas was 40 cents; and
- A dozen eggs cost 45 cents.

AND, SOME THINGS THAT WOULD MARK THE FUTURE IN WAYS UNKNOWABLE AT THE TIME:
- The World Trade Center in New York became the tallest building in the world; and
- Monica Lewinsky was born on July 23rd.

Other Restaurants (both near and far)

HERE IS A SNAPSHOT OF SOME OF THE EATERIES IN OPERATION
AT THE TIME: DURHAM'S CULINARY LANDSCAPE.

STEAKHOUSES:

- HARTMAN'S STEAKHOUSE (1703 East Geer Street)

   Hartman's was in the eastern part of Durham County, not within city limits. For some reason the fact that the parking lot was on one side of the road and the restaurant on the other has somehow stuck with me. It may be that the road was somewhat busy and you had the sense that you needed to cross it quickly. There was a pond on the back side which had swans. They were famous for their steaks (of course), their wedge salad: iceberg lettuce topped with blue cheese dressing, and their fried banana peppers. I never got the latter two of those offerings.

- THE ANGUS BARN (Hwy 70, Raleigh)

   The Angus Barn is halfway between Durham and Raleigh out near the airport. It is still open for business and has a solid reputation for serving well-prepared cuts of choice beef. It was always an expensive place to have dinner. I have been there twice, both involving wedding rehearsal dinners.

CHINESE: THE FOUR SEAS (300 W. Morgan Street)

Martha Maiden introduced me to The Four Seas. She tells me it was where she learned to cook. It quickly became a favorite place for my celebrations, including birthday dinners. As a treat, I would order the sweet plum wine for dessert. I remember they served stir-fried romaine lettuce under their chicken and cashew dish which seemed very exotic. The building was torn down to make way for the high rise office building, The Durham Centre.

NANCE'S CAFETERIA (West Dillard Street); formally called A.B. Morris

I have quite a few references on my calendars to eating at Nance's. The Cafeteria was on a side street facing one of the tobacco factories. They served BBQ, fried chicken, Brunswick stew, hushpuppies, and sweet tea. It was a place where students, businessmen, lawyers, and the factory workers from across the street all frequented.

DELI: THE IVY ROOM: (1000 Main Street)

When I did go out, the restaurant I most favored was The Ivy Room – only two blocks down Main Street from Duke's East Campus. This was where I drank my first beer (a Heineken) which I hated, ordered my first mixed drink (a Black Russian) which I liked, and where Tom and I shared a celebratory lunch after finding out we were pregnant with Marielle; we got burgers.

The Ivy Room was a staple of Durham: part delicatessen with cheesecake flown in daily from New York City alongside of Southern style comfort food which appealed to everyone. Everything was on the menu from Ruebens and Roast Beef Sandwiches to Open-faced Hot Turkey Sandwiches with stuffing and gravy, Grilled Swiss on Rye and baskets of Fried Chicken. It also included a small retail area which stocked items not found elsewhere. I remember buying their cans of artichokes and capers while Tom would buy beautiful cigarettes with colored paper wrappings. There were two hardworking waitresses who gave a certain authenticity and distinctiveness to the place: Frieda, completely down to earth, and Dot who carried her head held high, her white bleached bouffant hair reaching up to heaven. I still remember walking back to Duke at night from the bus station with a sense of fear at the loneliness of the streets after dark. Upon making it to The Ivy Room I would take a big sigh of relief, knowing I was almost back to campus.

PIZZA: ANNAMARIA'S (107 Albemarle Street)

Right around the corner from The Ivy Room, on Albemarle Street, was Annamaria's, known as Bat's, a pizza parlor in a converted small frame white house. It was a laid back, family operation. Known for its collection of comic books, a guitar Bat sometimes played, and the honor system in which you told the cashier what you had ordered at the end of your meal.

DOWN HOME SOUTHERN:

- HONEY'S (2702 Guess Road)

  Honey's was the favorite place for Lise and Charlie and members of the Mobile City Band to go and unwind after a gig. I only went with them once. Besides being a homebody, I generally worked weekend brunch shifts and needed to get home for some sleep.

- THE ROCKWOOD DAIRY BAR (University Drive)

  The Dairy Bar began with its connection to the dairy farm and bottling plant on James Street which operated from 1890, beginning with the Ward family, through the 1990s under various iterations and names (Lakewood, Longmeadow, Pet, Pine State, and finally Flav-o-rich). You could get any of their sandwiches grilled and they had the creamiest ice cream ever. My favorite flavor was Peppermint, a light shade of pink with finely crushed peppermint candies folded in.

- AND IN THE BE-IT-EVER-SO-HUMBLE CATEGORY: Many hot dog "establishments" including: Hazel's Hotdogs, Amos n'

Andy's, and King's.

There Were Also Places I Liked in Chapel Hill:

- ### The Rathskeller (Franklin Street)

  To get into the Rat, you first descended a steep set of concrete steps into Amber Alley. Once inside the darkened seating area, you felt like you had gone someplace far away. You could have been in the cellar of a European castle. Steaks were served sizzling on the pans in which they had been cooked.

- ### Tijuana Fats (Rosemary Street)

  Fats was the first Mexican place I had ever been to and probably where I was introduced to guacamole. Again, the approach to the restaurant was memorable: its entrance was down a narrow, dimly-lit alley off of Rosemary Street.

And Farther Afield, The Golden Temple (Washington, DC)

Prior to the opening, Elmer, Mary, and I took a trip up to DC to visit a couple of restaurants as a field trip and mini-break. We stayed with friends of Elmer's who lived there. The restaurant I remember most vividly was The Golden Temple, an Indian vegetarian restaurant. Its full name was The Golden Temple Conscious Cookery. It had opened in 1970, as part of a community led by Yogi Bhajan, who followed the teachings of Kundalini Yoga which he believed helped people live healthy, happy, and holy lives. We ate a fine dinner and had a very engaging waitress who took us down to the belly of the basement kitchen where they were making a huge batch of hummus. Shortly after we got back to Durham, that very waitress, Honorah Domizio, showed up at our front door. She came with an offer to work, having just moved to Durham with her husband, Dan, newly enrolled in Duke's Physician's Assistant Program. We took the presence of Honorah as a Good Portent, A Lucky Indicator, and we were very encouraged that she had come to join us.

And Now for Something Completely Different

These days, whenever I mention co-founding Somethyme, the response is one of delight and surprise. "That was where my wife and I had our first date." "That was my favorite place to go." "What was that egg sandwich called?"

We rapidly became an institution, a town favorite, a destination. We were one of the first "different" kind of restaurants to appear: we were not a seafood place (although we served fish), not a BBQ joint, not a deli, not a pizza parlor, not a Chinese restaurant, not a steakhouse. These were the kind of restaurants Durham had in spades. With Elmer's connections bringing in the curious and generally supportive first customers and Mary's good food turning them into regulars, we had waiting lines right away.

There was a wave of change coming to the culinary seascape, and we were riding it: a new food philosophy was developing. Food itself, each ingredient, was starting to become worthy of consideration. Was it organic? Was it fresh? Was it local? How was it processed? Was it good for you?

Our ingredients and vendor choices reflected this. We chose Lindley Mills' organic whole wheat over Pillsbury bleached white flour; Texan Lundberg short grain brown rice over Uncle Ben's; Deaf Smith peanut butter over Skippy; cheddar from the New York cheese maker Kutter's instead of Kraft. We made things from scratch and presented them artfully. We were an early local manifestation of the growing national movement that changed how we shopped, what we bought, how we cooked, and what we ate.

Two important recipe books we consulted were *The Tassajara Bread Book* (1970) and *The Vegetarian Epicure* (1972). The former was written in the late 1960's by a young Zen student named Edward Espe Brown, who lived and worked at a Zen retreat named Tassajara, in Monterey County, California. *The Vegetarian Epicure* was written by Anna Thomas when she was just a college student. This book was extremely influential nationally as an early unapologetic proponent of great tasting vegetarian food. Unlike, *Diet for a Small Planet* published in 1971 by Frances Moore Lappé, a true pioneer and advocate for a change in the way we eat, Anna Thomas offered recipes with a creative flare – food you could serve to company, not just standard fare for family dining. For sure, it influenced me. I still use her recipes. Her German Apple Pancake has become our family's Christmas and Easter holiday breakfast. The Corn and Cheddar Cheese Chowder, a winter's dinner favorite. She stated her idealistic embrace of vegetarianism in her introduction: "Good food is a celebration of life, and it seems absurd to me that in celebrating life we should take life."

For the times, the early 1970s, Durham was not unlike other cities in the country. Statistically, on a national level, steakhouses were the most popular type of restaurant and the most frequently ordered item was a hamburger. The options were between broad categories (pizza vs. Chinese) rather than the niche operations of today with chefs who have graduated from culinary schools.

What Durham had were the "tried and trues" – places that had been serving a standard unchanging fare to the populace for years, for decades. But the times, they were a-changing, as Bob Dylan was proclaiming. People's tastes were beginning to broaden, a bit of what-if and why-not started to permeate the same-old, same-old atmosphere. Somethyme burst into this staid scene like an upstart hipster (although, I have to say, back then we were thought of as the laid-back hippie). We had no interest in recreating the readily available. Our menu would be a full-throated alternative to the steak and potatoes, BBQ and slaw, fried chicken and french fries commonly offered.

Some famous examples of the newly emerging restaurant ethic were: Alice Waters' Chez Panisse founded in Berkeley, California in 1971 and the legendary collective Moosewood in Ithaca, New York which began, like us, in 1973, but unlike us is still in operation.

Locally, Wellspring Grocery is an example of this change in philosophy in the category of grocery markets. In 1978, Lex and Ann Alexander began planning for a grocery store that would be different from both the existing national or regional chains and the neighborhood mom & pop markets. They wanted to offer produce and grocery items that were well sourced (researched using high standards of quality), great-tasting, and nutritious. They wanted to encourage consumers to be more connected with the food they purchased and ate. Their first store, right around the corner from us (up a block on Knox and Ninth Streets), opened in 1981 and was completely vegetarian. In 1986, when they moved to a larger space a couple blocks away on Markham and Ninth Streets, fish, poultry, and meat were added. They opened a second store in Chapel Hill in 1990, and in 1991 Wellspring merged with Whole Foods Market (begun in 1978 and whose originators were considered compatriots by Lex and Ann). There was a kinship between Wellspring and Somethyme as we shared the same philosophy about food. Over the years, many Somethyme staff (including both me and Tom) became Wellspringers/Whole Fooders, and I'm proud of that.

Ken Dawson and Libby Outlaw's Maple Springs Farm is an example of this change in the grower and farmers market world. We were among Ken and Libby's first tomato customers. This is how Ken describes, on his website, his entry into his life-long work as a grower:

I first began growing vegetables using organic methods in 1972. What began as a backyard household garden evolved into a passion and a career. Through study and practice, I became convinced that there was a better way to farm than the conventional methods I saw being advocated and practiced. I became solidly committed to demonstrating the viability of farming practices that improve, rather than deplete the soil, that encourage a diverse ecosystem on the farm which results in a system of checks and balances among insect species; and yields safe, nutritious foods while not unnecessarily exposing farm workers, consumers or the environment to toxic chemicals.

Ken was one of the founding vendors of the Carrboro Farmers Market (the first of our markets) in 1978 and is a pillar in our local farming community today.

The Farm to Fork movement and the Slow Foods are recent outgrowths of the "new," maybe old by now, food scene. What began as a wave in the 1970s turned into a tsunami. Even national grocery store chains now offer organics, and it is common to see restaurants cite the local producers from whom they purchase eggs, cheese, meat, and produce. I guess the fact that Whole Foods was acquired by Amazon summarizes the last fifty years: what began as a food revolution has become completely mainstream.

Welcome to SomeThyme

Our restaurant is a meeting place for people who love to cook, serve, and eat fine natural foods. Our vocation is to cook and serve consciously and creatively for your pleasure and health. Our baked foods are prepared daily from organically grown grains and seasonings, while our entrees and sandwiches are made from fresh vegetables and natural cheeses. Some of our foods, such as sugar, cream cheese, coffee, and alcohol are not necessary for a healthy diet; consequently these items are offered as options to our basic menu.

SomeThyme is dedicated to the restoration of the natural, harmonious balance between persons and the earth. Situated on the edge of a collapsing nutritional and ecological system, we are a part of the growing exodus of persons and institutions back through unquestioned habit and abuse to a future where life may instead be nurtured, celebrated, and shared in peace. We invite you to join us on that journey.

There was so much going on in 1973: Women's Rights, the Black Power Movement, the Anti-War Movement, a growing awareness and concern for the health of the earth, Farm Worker Rights and Boycotts, a growing Anti-Nuclear sentiment, Voting Rights. We approached the issues at hand with a call to community and a pledge to do what we could as individuals and as a business to live with others in mind. Somethyme deliberately placed itself in the thick of the political arena, trying to be and act with a radical awareness of our place in history. We wanted to shoulder the burdens that were ours to bear. We didn't shrink from putting our mission and political beliefs on the menu, front and center, for anyone and everyone to read. I loved that about us.

As much as I try to remember what was going on back then, I find that I cannot without looking back through the lens of the present. The issues today are not dissimilar from those we faced back then and are, if anything, amplified. It saddens me to read our welcoming statement now, so hopeful in intent, as I consider the current state of the world. Rather than things improving, as we so clearly envisioned, things have gotten worse. 1973 was a heady time because we thought real change was possible and possibly imminent. We thought that if each of us did our own small part, we could address the challenges and accomplish great things. But sadly, maybe tragically, we have edged ever closer to that "collapsing ecological system" and the hope for a "harmonious balance" may no longer even be feasible. Roe vs. Wade has been overturned and as of October 2021, 19 states have enacted 33 laws that will make it harder for Americans to vote. By every metric, we live more uneasily with, and in greater suspicion of, each other than ever before, be it with our families, co-workers, or neighbors. In the intervening 50 years, we have found that Justice, Mercy, Love, and Peace are not easily achieved. But as Somethyme began to take shape, each of us – Elmer, Mary, and I – were excited about the prospect of starting a business that had ideals at its heart.

We opened officially on Wednesday, October 17, 1973 after taking a practice run for friends and supporters the night before. My mother wrote in her diary on October 21, reporting on a conversation with me right after the opening:

Mary said they were doing a big business – people were waiting in line to get in. So far they have had enough food for everyone. Don [my brother, a freshman then at Duke] *came on Thursday for dinner with 4 or 5 friends. He got the baked fish with lemon sauce and said it was good. She has been working 15 hours a day but feels good and is enjoying it. Everybody is working well together.*

Other than it being a full-blown adrenaline rush, my only distinct memory is that I sang the traditional song "900 Miles" a cappella following the rehearsal dinner to those who were still there, and I remember the dining area being packed. After singing, I went over to the ledge in front of the windows, sat down, and melted into tears. It did seem like we had come 900 miles in the span of just a few months and we were starting to get the idea that there would be untold miles yet to go. We finished Pre-Day One exuberant, blessedly ignorant that Somethyme would have 4,459 remaining days in its life: Open Every Day except Monday, from 11:00 a.m. straight through to midnight.

Our Menu

"Serving Fine Natural Foods for the People"

Our very first menu included a couple of Mary's signature dishes, which would be on every menu we ever had. The MSB – so called from the initials of her name: Mary Staples Bacon (obviously Mary was predestined to be a food wizard), was $1.60 and the Beanburger was 95 cents. I still make the MSB for dinner from time to time at home: an open-faced, layered sandwich starting with a slice of whole wheat bread spread with mustard (edge to edge), a fried egg (with the egg mostly cooked but slightly runny), sliced tomatoes (home-growns are the best), black pepper, sliced avocado, Spike seasoning (generously sprinkled), mayonnaise, alfalfa sprouts, and then placed under the broiler to melt the sliced mozzarella cheese on top. You could order a half portion or a whole. The whole was actually was two of what I just described. I could never eat a whole one, but many many people did and then would top it off with a piece of ginger cheesecake. We never counted calories at Somethyme.

The Beanburger was not something you can recreate in your home kitchen, or at least not without a lot of trouble, fuss, and mess. Soybeans were pressure cooked with crushed tomatoes, spices (garlic powder, basil, thyme, marjoram, chili powder, black pepper), and tamari. Then the thickened soft beans were drained through a china cap, "tossed" until as much liquid as possible had been forced out (this was what made the Beanburger so hard to make), then schmushed and combined with oats and sesame seeds as a binder. A weekly dreaded task.

The stately Heather Mountain (served with bread, and choice of soup or salad) was $2.95 and amazing to behold. This was the first dish Mary previewed for Elmer and me, at a dinner at her house prior to the opening. Its presentation was striking: a split piping-hot baked potato smothered with sautéed mushrooms and onions and topped with sour cream; the potato was encircled by slices of avocado and tomato arranged on a bed of alfalfa sprouts and drizzled with blue cheese dressing. I did not reveal, at the time, how much I hated mushrooms and blue cheese. Somehow I ate the whole thing. Even though this was something I would never eat again, I could, intellectually, appreciate its mystique.

The other entrees offered were the Middle Kingdom Vegetable Dish (fresh vegetables baked in a tarragon broth, served over brown rice, and topped with melted mozzarella) for $2.25; Eggplant Parmigiana for 2.65; and Savory Carolina Fish (a broiled filet basted in a ginger-soy, lemon-butter, or Malaysian curry sauce) served with browned potatoes and a vegetable for $2.65. The vegetable was often Elmer's specialty: sautéed green beans with garlic and sherry. By the second menu (a delightful, whimsical, and artsy creation for the summer drawn by Marilyn Roaf), Chinese Sauteed Vegetables and Shrimp Creole had replaced the Eggplant Parmigiana and the fish.

We also had the Morning Star, a composed entrée salad, consisting of a base of shredded carrots and sprouts circling the bowl, a plop of cottage cheese in the center, sliced apples radiating out from the cottage cheese, and then the whole thing topped with raisins, nuts, and toasted sunflower seeds and dressed with Umeboshi Plum Dressing. The dressing recipe was a gift from Elizabeth Anderson of The Wildflower Kitchen in Chapel Hill. For the uninitiated, umeboshi plums are a pickled plum of Japanese origin. You had to make sure all the plums had their seed removed before putting them in the blender. The dressing contained soy oil, cider vinegar, light honey, water, raw onion, salt, garlic powder, white pepper, ginger powder, chervil, eggs and the pitted plums. Here is a memory Wicca Paull shared about a mishap when she was making the Umeboshi Plum Dressing:

One time I was making the umeboshi plum dressing in the industrial blender.

Helen Hancock was next to me kneading bread. And the top blew off the blender. Helen and I were covered in plums and oil and all the other ingredients. I couldn't see because my glasses were coated – so I could not find the lid. Helen and I were laughing hysterically. Those were the good old days.

Lemon Tamari Dressing was like none I had ever known. For one, it included fresh vegetables (onions, green peppers, and celery). After the vegetables were blended into pulp, more normal ingredients were added: fresh lemon juice, soy oil, tahini, garlic powder, white pepper, tamari, safflower oil, and a little honey. It had the bite of onion, the salt of tamari, the sweetness of the green pepper and honey, and the sour of lemon juice. It was a hit.

The apple pie on the dessert menu was a gift from Duke graduate, Gary Wein. I can still hear him telling me how to make pie dough – the description of when you know you have added enough butter (slightly damp), how it looks (crumbly corn meal), how it feels (kinda holding its shape if you slightly pressed a handful), how it smells (buttery sweet). He also came and gave us an omelette technique lesson prior to opening. By 1973, Gary was already a highly respected chef and caterer having founded The Savory Fare Catering Company.

The seasoning Spike was an important secret weapon Mary brought with her from California. Elmer and I had certainly never heard of it before. Spike was created by the nutritionist Gayelord Hauser. Still available at specialty grocery stores, it contains 39 different dried vegetables and seasonings: salt crystals (earth and sea), hydrolyzed soy protein, soy granules, toasted onion, nutritional yeast, garlic, orange powder, dill, kelp, horseradish, mustard flour, orange and lemon peel, celery granules and powder, sweet green and red bell peppers, parsley flakes, celery root powder, white pepper, turmeric, rosehips, summer savory, onion powder, mushroom powder, coriander, fenugreek, basil, cayenne pepper, spinach powder, cloves, cumin, ginger, marjoram, oregano, thyme, tarragon, cinnamon, safflower, paprika, tomato, rosemary, and ground celery seed.

This spice seasoning is amazing on avocados. It is what made the MSB taste so good. The seasoning combination strikes me as being very inclusive. It contains fruits and vegetables, salt from the earth and salt from the sea, Mediterranean herbs and Asian spices, flowers and mushrooms, sweet and savory flavors. Maybe it is a recipe of how we can all live together. It was not available in bulk, so we bought it in individual-sized bottles with a red cap. It was a joy to sprinkle the spice from a freshly opened bottle and a frustration when it clumped together because of humidity, as it was prone to do.

We had wanted to offer beer and wine but, initially, were prevented from doing so. Clements Funeral Service registered a complaint with the Alcohol Board Commission, anticipating double-the-trouble should there be two establishments serving alcohol in close proximity to them (The Top Hat and us). The ABC hearing in Raleigh on November 30, 1973 sided with them, but the Durham City Council overturned their ruling on January 4, 1974 and granted us a license. The fact that we were not attempting to be a bar but a restaurant that served alcohol to enhance the diner's enjoyment (and perhaps the fact that one of the owners was a Methodist minister) won the day.

Our prices seem so cheap now: a cup of coffee was 20 cents; hot chocolate, 25 cents; omelettes started at $1.10 for plain going up to $2.10 for everything (cheese, mushrooms, tomatoes, onions, and green peppers); tuna salad sandwich: $1.15; a cup of soup: 35 cents; small side salad: 60 cents; apple pie: 40 cents or with ice cream, 60 cents; raisin bread pudding 35 cents. How did we ever make money?

By today's standards our opening menu was not sophisticated or extensive. Four entrees on the dinner menu. Grilled cheese on the lunch menu. But we built a solid reputation for hearty and imaginative soups, fresh bread, good salad dressings, and homemade desserts. At the time, it was enough and there was nothing like it in town. It was fresh, tasty, and not expensive. It was a friendly and laid back place. The staff were your friends who just happened to work there. You could go by yourself and not feel out of place. Rich people came and poor people came and were served with an egalitarian spirit; both left satisfied. We were more than a restaurant: we were a community that offered community, and in no time we became an integral part of people's lives.

Within These Four Walls

We had always hoped that Somethyme would provide food for both body and soul. That soul offering was to be in the form of art, music, poetry, and discourse. We wanted to be supportive of the arts and to offer a place where ideas could be nurtured and flourish. We weren't sure how we would go about that, but we dedicated wall space for hanging art; our business hours were suitably extended to accommodate music and spoken word performance; and the physical space itself could host events for organizations or people we supported. We built a stage, bought sound equipment (microphones and stands, speakers, and a mixing board) and offered a late night menu to encourage attendance. We must have succeeded because Georgann Eubanks describes Somethyme as "the cultural heartbeat of the community."

We had revolving month-long art shows from the beginning including works by Nancy Tuttle May, Russell Rigsbee, Sue Sneddon, Caroline Vaughan, and Emily Weinstein.

Let me take a moment and write about one of those artists, the late Sue Sneddon. Sue had a multi-layered relationship with the restaurant (as did many of our artists and musicians). Somethyme hosted her first solo show. Hung in 1979, it would be followed by four others including one during the Seventh Street years in 1989. In addition to showing her luminous landscapes and seascapes, she created illustrations for our advertising, especially those we ran in *The Independent Weekly*, a local publication with progressive news, culture, music, and commentary for the Triangle. She was also a percussionist with the Rhythm & Blues band I was/am in (Lise Uyanik and Mobile City Band), probably our most extroverted member on stage – always wearing an infectious love-of-life smile.

The 1979 Sue Sneddon Art Opening. Sue, on the left standing; Georgann Eubanks on the left in the booth; photo provided by Nance Sneddon

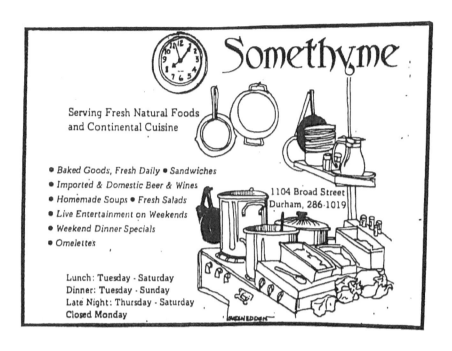

Somethyme

Serving Fresh Natural Foods
and Continental Cuisine

- *Baked Goods, Fresh Daily • Sandwiches*
- *Imported & Domestic Beer & Wines*
- *Homemade Soups • Fresh Salads*
- *Live Entertainment on Weekends*
- *Weekend Dinner Specials*
- *Omelettes*

1104 Broad Street
Durham, 286-1019

Lunch: Tuesday - Saturday
Dinner: Tuesday - Sunday
Late Night: Thursday - Saturday
Closed Monday

Somethyme Restaurant

Serving Fresh Natural Foods
and Continental Cuisine

- *Baked Goods, Fresh Daily • Sandwiches*
- *Imported & Domestic Beer and Wines*
- *Homemade Soups • Fresh Salads*
- *Live Entertainment on Weekends*
- *Weekend Dinner Specials*
- *Omelettes*

Lunch: Tuesday - Saturday
Dinner: Tuesday - Sunday
Late Night: Thursday - Saturday
Closed Monday

Under staff member Aden Field's leadership, Sunday night's "Somethyme Voices" flourished. In addition to weekly poetry readings, we hosted classical string quartets and woodwind quintets, and the most ambitious undertaking of all: a theatrical performance of the *Spoon River Anthology* in the fall of 1985 with a cast of eleven (including former Bluebird owner Nona McKee). When Aden left in 1976, no one took up the "Somethyme Voices" banner.

Throughout the years, we were proud to host nationally known politicians and activists to our humble stage. To Elmer's delight, Philip Berrigan, the peace and civil rights activist and Roman Catholic priest, accepted an invitation to speak. He came on a Thursday night in 1975. We also held fundraisers for local and national candidates. The ecologist and one of the founders of the environmental movement, Barry Commoner, came in 1980 as the presidential candidate of the Citizens Party. His work on the issue of radioactive fallout from nuclear weapons was a major reason why the Nuclear Test Ban Treaty passed. (Our fundraiser didn't do much to increase his visibility; he only got .27 percent of the vote nationally.)

Right from the beginning, we knew that we were not going to serve Gallo wine, table grapes, or iceberg lettuce. These were farm products that were being boycotted in support of Cesar Chavez's United Farm Worker strike. We were probably never going to sell Gallo wine or iceberg lettuce, but the grapes would have been nice. Over the years we hosted many popular benefits for the United Farm Workers. We made lots of enchiladas and lots of rice and beans, opened the restaurant on normally-closed Monday nights, served capacity crowds, and gave all the proceeds to the UFW. We also hosted benefits for the "Stop the Shearon Harris Nuclear Power Plant" a plant which began construction in 1978 about 30 miles from Durham.

But being a place for music probably best exemplified our commitment to the arts. Music expressed the soul of the restaurant and was where my own soul found a home. We became a place, maybe even the place, for music in Durham. Early on, Len (and sadly, I don't remember his last name – someone from the Duke community) stepped in and offered to host audition/open mic nights and do our bookings. When he moved away, Charlie Ebel (who would become my music buddy) took over that role. We scheduled music Wednesdays through Saturdays with an audition/open mic night on Tuesdays. Wednesdays or Thursdays (depending on the year) became jazz nights.

Jack LeSueur; photo provided by Patti LeSueur

For compensation, we offered a meal and a glass of wine or beer to the musician(s); the cashier passed the hat. Sometimes we guaranteed the tips. We advertised our schedule both internally and in the local papers. For the most part the music was guitar-based folk, blues, country, bluegrass, old timey, originals, or jazz. These groups drew a listening and attentive audience. We were never short of musicians wanting to play on our stage – many of whom came from our talented staff.

Another of Sue Sneddon's illustrations of and for Somethyme

After a busy dinner shift it was relaxing to hang out, have a cappuccino, beer, or glass of wine, listen to the music, and unwind. I regularly stayed after a dinner shift or came in especially to hear to the smooth guitar and vocal blend of Jack & Patti LeSueur, the songwriting of Ty Stephens, the driving country-flavored quartet of Home Across the Road, and the rollicking Nee Ningy Band with their high-energy sonic blend of fiddle, mandolin, washtub base, and shouted vocals. On these nights when the latter two were playing, the place would be packed with whooping and hollering and all-around good cheer.

Elizabeth Cotten was the most famous musician who ever performed at Somethyme. And, what an honor that was. This opportunity came from George Holt and Lanier Rand (a former employee and housemate of Elmer's). George was the producer of Durham's first

Folk Life Festival which morphed into the Festival for the Eno that still goes on. Elizabeth sang her familiar songs including "Freight Train" and "Shake Sugaree" to a rapt and appreciative audience.

Elizabeth Cotten; photo taken by Bill Gaither at the restaurant, September 28, 1975

Teresa Trull was a local who would go on to have a national reputation in women's music. She toured with Chris Williamson, whose cassette tapes we wore out during service hours. As a teenager, Teresa was the lead singer in Rocky Kramm's Ed's Bush Band, which may have been the first band that ever played at the restaurant. I always felt like Teresa was someone who could endow Somethyme with enough soul and good vibes to weather any storm. She had that kind of positive energy.

Teresa Trull; photo courtesy of Lew Wardell

For myself, the stage is where my music life and my Somethyme life intertwined; the restaurant became a principal performance venue for me. It was here that Charlie Ebel, Lise Uyanik, and I began singing together. My strongest memories of the restaurant are ones that come from our performances. Some old recordings keep them vivid in my mind as well. Covers of "Travelin' Shoes," "Two More Bottles of Wine," "Leavin' Louisiana," and "O Freedom" are first and foremost Somethyme songs. We came together at Somethyme, because of Somethyme, and we matured as performers on that stage.

Although in my Duke days I had solo gigs, my musical journey truly began to take shape and solidify when I started to play music with

Charlie. He and I were in the same class at Duke. As I recall, we knew of, or at least were aware of, each other, but it was through Elmer that introductions were formally made. Charlie was in Elmer's circle of friends and so he started to become a familiar person to me. The first time we played music together was at the wedding of staffers Barry Jacobs and Libby McKeithen on May 5, 1974. Their wedding was at an old farm house in Orange County that you had to drive on dirt roads to get to. It was raining some and we both sought shelter in a barn stall. We had our guitars and began trading songs. Our playing and singing together felt and sounded natural. We played songs like James Taylor's "Sweet Baby James" and John Denver's "Country Roads." A little over a month later, on June 24 after a dinner at Elmer's, we played together again and followed that up with our first public performance (at Somethyme, of course).

Two years went by and then in June of 1976, I started making notes in my calendar of someone named Lise Uyanik, about going to hear her sing and play. Lise was born and raised in Raleigh and was making the coffeehouse rounds with her folk and bluesy material ("Cry Me a River," "Everybody's Crying Mercy"). She started playing at Somethyme. Her voice was sultry and soulful. Her eyes were sultry and soulful. She captivated everyone, including Charlie. In the summer of 1977, the three of us started to sing together: we became a trio. Shortly after, Rob McIntyre joined us on bass and vocals and we became a quartet. We never had a proper name – we mostly used our last names, sometimes we used both our first and last names, and the order of the names was never consistent. Because Lise wanted to start a Rhythm & Blues band, in 1978 she and Charlie formed the Mobile City Band. Along with Shannon Dancy (who worked at Pyewacket), I became a Mobilette, a backing vocalist, singing when they played in-town gigs. Charlie and Lise got married; I sang at their wedding, and the band played at their reception. Mobile City emerged as the unofficial house band of both Somethyme and Seventh Street.

The Work:
Bookkeeping, Baking, and Cooking

BOOKKEEPING

Elmer, Mary and I had thought a lot about the menu, our hours, hiring, scheduling, pay rates, and the like. But we didn't give much thought to bookkeeping as an on-going task. A couple of weeks into being open, the staff began turning in little pieces of paper with how many hours they had worked. Although Elmer did the payroll initially, starting in February 1974, Aden Field, with his accounting background, agreed to train me as a bookkeeper.

His first bookkeeping instruction was this: get a bound ledger book. Now, a ledger book is a huge book. I don't know where mine went but it was certainly not lost given its size: the pages were 11 x 17 inches. Aden was a good and patient teacher, explaining the double entry method, how to calculate payroll and payroll taxes, how sales tax worked, how to code income and expenses. Through his training I discovered what one of my contributions to the partnership would be: I became the bookkeeper. Maybe it was in my genes. My paternal grandfather had been an accountant and even as a child I was allowed to keep the purse and track our spending during family camping trips. I liked the work and have been a bookkeeper as one of my work personas ever since.

At that time, there was no such thing as a payroll service, Intuit or Quickbooks software, or even an Excel spreadsheet. The tools at my disposal were ledger sheets, a pencil (not even a mechanical one!), an eraser, a "desk-sized" 10-key calculator, and the printed booklets of the federal and state withholding tax schedules. We adopted a bi-weekly pay period. I would set myself up in one of the booths, if possible, or in the tiny desk in the back hallway if not, to do payroll. I had to list everyone who worked that pay period, add up and record their hours from their time sheets, multiply them by their rate of pay for a gross wage, apply and record the Social Security percentage tax, reference their declared exemptions, consult the tax schedules for their federal and state withholding taxes, and come up with a net pay figure. Then I would have to make sure the whole thing balanced. When it did, I could write out the individual checks. This process took hours and hours. Now when I do payroll for clients, it takes a fraction of the time; I love using that almighty "enter" key!

On a daily basis, cashiers rang up the customers' tickets, item by item, at the cash register. Having quick and accurate fingers was an asset. When we first opened, credit cards were not in use so customers paid in cash or wrote checks. To start making sense of our sales, we developed daily summaries to make sure that the money we deposited equaled, or at least was close to, the money we thought we should have. From the daily summaries came weekly summaries; from the weekly summaries came monthly reports. We tracked lunch sales vs. dinner sales vs. late-night sales; food vs. alcohol; entrees ordered within shifts. We began to be able to compare months-worth and later, years-worth of data.

Very early we partnered with an accounting firm. I would turn over our books to them: the payroll records, the reconciled bank statements, sales reports, and the coded check register. They would turn them into Profit and Loss Statements. Our first accountant, Steve Neighbors, had an office on King Street in Hillsborough. Driving with Mary, or later Martha Maiden, along Highway 70W, turning left onto St. Mary's Road, and then right on King Street was an enjoyable getting-out-of-the-place activity. It was and is such a pretty drive. Part of me still sees that route, which is one I take frequently, through the eyes of that memory.

Taking on the books for the restaurant was something that I would shoulder for 17 years. Who knew? I think doing this quiet work, which I enjoyed, must have provided the ballast for the other work that was physically demanding and emotionally turbulent. Every week, I had a chance to sit down and work the numbers. This was a puzzle, but it was a puzzle I could solve. I would work until I found the error or the oversight or double entry, until the columns added up properly. I could do this and call the job done. I could do this and say I understood what was on the page; I could state with complete confidence that it was accurate. It wasn't about whether we made or lost money (although I did care about that); it was just a series of mathematical calculations; it was either right or wrong. It wasn't about how to state a criticism that wouldn't hurt someone's feelings; these were just numbers. It wasn't about how my back might be hurting from lifting too many bags of flour; it was the happy smile smiled in private, the pat on the back I gave myself, the victory lap I took though no one might be there to observe it.

BAKING

The transition from baking for my household to baking for the restaurant was, principally, one of scale. At home, one batch of bread was eight pounds in weight and produced four loaves which would last at least one week. Now each day, it was routine to make two sixteen pound batches. We did not have a big Hobart mixer for the dough making. We had the strength of our arms; we had large stainless-steel bowls, big whisks, and long sturdy wooden bread paddles. A batch began with 13 cups of water to which was added a blend of honey and molasses as sweeteners, yeast, soy oil, salt, and poppy seeds for a little crunch and visual appeal. This whole wheat recipe included a bit of unbleached flour to give it some lightness. You could tell who baked the bread by the bread itself. Even though we all used the same recipe, each baker had something of a signature embedded in the final product.

Mary (who also had bake shifts) was known for coming into the kitchen, and if she found bread dough rising in a bowl, she'd give it a gentle pat and say "smooth as a baby's bottom." She loved saying that.

The baking station was on the left back side of the kitchen. There were big barrels for the whole wheat flour, unbleached flour, and turbinado sugar, each holding 150 pounds; a rack for smaller containers of yeast, baking powder, baking soda, and baking spices. The soybean oil came in 5-gallon-sized plastic jugs, the honey and molasses in 5-gallon buckets. It always felt like we were preparing for a feast. The apple pie shift began at 5:00 in the morning and the bread shift one hour later. On Mondays, when we were closed, we had special baking shifts for bagels, English muffins, and cheesecakes.

The bread baker also made the other desserts: cookies, cakes, custards, bread pudding, and pies. This was another transition for me. I was and am primarily a bread baker. I became a skilled pie dough maker. But being a confectionery baker was never my strong suit. If at all possible, I left the Chocolate Cake to Jeannie Gamble, the Rum Cake to Alice Glenn, and the Pirate Cake to Tom.

I loved my bake shifts, so I guess it is no surprise that those were the shifts I held onto the longest. The last shifts I worked (in 1989, seven months pregnant) were weekend brunches. I especially loved making English muffins, I still do. The bake shifts were lower pressure than the cook positions. There were fewer people around. You were basically alone in the kitchen to start with. You could choose what desserts to bake, as long as you ended up with an assortment of offerings. And, there was a variety in the actual tasks. As a brunch baker, I would make whole wheat bread, French bread, biscuits, quiche, griddle-cake batter, and cinnamon buns. And, oh my goodness, those cinnamon buns were good.

The smell of bread baking wafting out into the seating area and out into the street via the exhaust fan was some good advertising. Now I try to imagine what those baking smells must have meant to the customers coming in for lunch or brunch. There is nothing like the smell of bread just out of the oven to stimulate an appetite. Yum. But there was something deeper than just "Yum" going on. The word "company," in fact, means "with bread." Sharing Bread is an ancient symbol of Peace and Kinship. Though we may not have been cognizant of the literal meaning of the word *company*, we were, in fact, embodying it. Offering fresh baked bread every day for our customers was one of the most important ways we had of *being* community and *being with* community.

Fresh baked bread meant that all the bread needed to be sliced. I was a very good slicer and I have no idea how many loaves of bread I have sliced over the years. Decades later, my customers at the Chapel Hill Farmer's Market used to watch in amazement when I sliced their bread. I have a steady hand, a sharp eye, and an even pace. I am like a machine. Every slice, the same as the one before or after. Slicing bread became a pleasure to me at Somethyme.

We had many bakers over the years, ones that made real contributions to our menu. Jeannie Cheeseman taught us how to make bagels and her delicious ginger cheesecakes (both honey ones and sugar ones) became standard dessert fare, Rachel Preston taught us how to make English muffins, Jane Collins contributed the genre of custards and, in particular, the coconut cream pie which became a favorite, and Jeannie Gamble made the best chocolate cake ever, AKA Jeannie's Chocolate Cake.

Some of my favorite desserts were the aforementioned Rum Cake and Pirate Cake as well as every type of cookie. We had awesome pies – who can forget the Blueberry Streusel? We welcomed bakers in from the community as star players, and as pinch hitters. Billy Stevens made gulab jamun for our Indian weekends and Deanna George made baklava for Greek weekends.

Rachel Preston's hands; photo by Jonathan Moss, October 1974

Baking was one of the more obvious places where we tried to match our ideology with what we produced. We wanted our baked items to be both good-tasting and good for you. The use of whole wheat flour vs. white flour and the use of honey, molasses, or turbinado sugar instead of processed sugar are good illustrations. We substituted turbinado for white sugar in our recipes. Turbinado comes from the first pressing of sugar cane and retains more of the plant's flavor and natural molasses. Its flavor is more nuanced and well-rounded than white sugar and its crystals are coarser and darker. In an early attempt to communicate our food practices and aspirations, we published a newsletter. The very first one was about baking. In it we said:

Many of our desserts are made with honey or molasses: gingerbread, cookies, bread pudding, and banana bread. Thus far, though, cheesecake and apple pie have been made with sugar. Until we can produce a pleasing cheesecake with honey, we will continue using sugar.

We did succeed in that quest for a honey cheesecake and a honey apple pie.

COOKING

I believe that the heart of the restaurant resided in the stove position, both the day stove shift and the dinner stove shift. In addition to working the lunch shift, the day stove made the sauces, the critical part of the entrees. These needed to be consistently well-made and uniform in quality. The stove, in particular, required timing and discernment since everything was individually cooked to order. There were so many second-to-second and minute-to-minute decisions the cook had to make about whether or not something was done or needed more time. And there were multiple tasks occurring at once: MSBs under the broiler, eggs on the griddle, stir fried vegetables in the wok, shrimp in the boil pot, and an omelette in the pan. You had to be totally focused and ready.

It was the hottest position to work. The kitchen was not air-conditioned. We did at some point install a big fan to keep the air moving, and there were small fans placed here and there. But they did little to combat the heat from the ovens, broiler, and stove eyes especially in the summer.

In the beginning, besides the baking at which I was proficient, my time was spent prepping and learning how to cook. I did not bring with me the knowledge needed to stove cook or short order. Despite living off-campus which meant cooking for myself and housemates, I was not a cook. I had average-college-student level cooking credentials. I made note in my calendars of the meals I cooked at Omega House and Knox Street, they were things like eggs and fried potatoes, hamburgers, spaghetti, stuffed peppers, tuna casserole. I had been an unambitious cook making unambitious meals. I came to the restaurant as a beginner. But once there, I was keen on learning and improving my skills.

Mary was a fine role model and is a great cook. She became highly regarded and deservedly so; shoot, she became a legend. Her flavors were thick yet distinct, sharp yet embracing. She had a way with sauces and salad dressings. She was always tweaking the recipes, moving them closer to the taste or texture she imagined. She loved sharing her creations. "Come and taste this!" was a common request, if not command.

I learned by watching her how to slice onions in half-moons or "a china cut" and how to rough chop or finely mince them. I learned by scrutinizing her recipes about spice families and how cumin is used in Mexican and Middle Eastern and African and Indian cuisines, each one with different partners. I learned how to chiffonade fresh basil leaves. I learned to love caramelized onions, how to make a cream sauce, how cornstarch thickens a sauce and then how the sauce clears once it boils. I learned how to be bold when making omelettes. As my proficiency and competence improved, I was able to handle actual cooking on the line.

My first shifts included baking, late-night cooking and clean-up, and a bar shift. The late-night cooking was very simple: toasting a bagel and the like. It enabled us to offer customers a little something to eat when they came in to listen to the music, as well as make sure things were cleaned up and tidy for the next day. The bar menu included carrot juice (made to order using a Champion juicer), smoothies, blended iced tea and juice drinks – all of which used the blender. It was a noisy bar!! I was surprised to see from my calendar that I had worked bar shifts in the beginning. One of my lines used to be "I never waited tables and I never tended bar." But, apparently, I did have bar shifts, so that part of my line is wrong. I stand by my statement that I was never a wait person.

I liked working the dinner shift from 5:00-9:00 (or 9:30 on the weekends). There was an abundance of food. The sauces set out on the steam table: Chinese Veggie Sauce aka CVS (tamari, garlic, and ginger flavored), Mornay (a rich white sauce with cheese and lemon), and the Indonesian Curry Sauce (tomato based with peanut butter, sautéed onions and lots of spices). Prepped vegetables for the wok stir fry, broccoli for the steamer, shelled shrimp for quick boiling, chopped ingredients for omelettes. I enjoyed shift work and the feeling of accomplishment from a job well done. The great camaraderie of restaurant work is well known and a real thing. All the pieces, all the jobs, all the people have to work together to make it happen.

The Restaurant as a Whole

One of the maxims in the restaurant world is that if you have a reliable dishwasher you can open for business. There is something to that. We had more transition in our dish and clean-up crew than any of the others. I got the nickname "Sudsy" because I had to fill in so often. But that said, we had a lion's share of stalwart dishwashers, especially Steve Darling, or as we sometimes called him, Dr. Dish, who held shifts longer than any other and approached the work with the mind of a philosopher.

I have a couple years of Cook's Notes in a three-ring binder; most are in my writing, some in Tom's from his time as a Kitchen Manager. They cover the end of 1984 through most of 1987. Running the kitchen and working in the kitchen required a massive amount of keeping up with things, checking off to-do lists. But the notes which cover both Somethyme and Seventh Street have a consistency to them. They are both filled with reminders to be nice to the waits, show consideration to the dish staff, take care of the food inventory, follow the damn recipe. There is so much detail in kitchen work, and it's all necessary and important – the tiniest mundane details were often the most important.

Kitchen Rules & Etiquette

Interactions:

- *Job performance and attitude are considered equal in importance. The kitchen is a stressful place to work both physically and emotionally. Everyone must allow space for the other person. Though the degrees of skill differ, no one job is more important than another, requiring the efforts of everyone to get the food out. This depends on the cooperation of the short order, stove, line, prep cook, the kitchen in general, and the front staff as well as transitions between shifts. This is the principle behind producing a high quality product and service. An egocentric or elitist attitude is destructive to the spirt of Somethyme.*

- *Because we all contribute to the product it is important that there be a constant striving for excellence. There must be a commitment made toward challenging the best from others and accepting challenge to bring forth the best from within. This kind of openness is not easy to maintain but it is the level on which we want the restaurant to operate.*

- *Communication on a shift, between shifts, and between days is very important. If you can't pass along information face to face, leave a note. If there is a problem, try to deal directly with the person involved. If this does not resolve the issue, speak to the kitchen manager. If it does not involve kitchen procedure, speak to our personnel manager.*

Consistency:

- *There is a standard for all the food prepared here. Deviation from this standard or inability to consistently reproduce this standard cannot be accepted. Examples include not following a recipe, over- or under-cooking food, wrong proportions or assemblage. If you are unsure, ask, don't guess. The customers depend on a consistent product as their basis for their ordering and patronage. The restaurant can't afford to lose its reputation for good food because of a cook's ignorance, carelessness, or attitude.*

Food Handling: Proper rotation of food is a key element to the kitchen functioning up to its potential. To this end:

- *All prepared food must be labeled, dated, and initialed*
- *Produce must be rotated when deliveries are received*
- *Use prepared food in order of its being made*
- *Do not mix batches of prepared food*
- *You are responsible for the food you serve. Be sure it is servable. Does it look good? Smell good? Taste good? Get a second opinion if you are unsure. If something is beginning to turn, discard it. This cannot be*

stressed enough.

- *The storage areas (walk-in, mezzanine, basement, freezers) need constant organizing to keep under control. Things must be consolidated – old on top of or in front of new. Put small volumes in small containers. Know where things are supposed to be and put them there.*

Hours: Every shift has its estimated hours listed on the master schedule. It is expected that you comply with these hours.

Subbing:

- *Getting subs for your shifts is your own responsibility. In times of sickness or personal emergency, you may enlist the help of management. The kitchen staff is small and everyone is totally dependent on each other for subs. We all need to be flexible in times of another's need. If someone consistently refuses to sub, his or her own job is jeopardized.*

- *People's needs and desires will be accommodated if at all possible but it may take time to work it out.*

- *All subs go on the calendar.*

Scheduling: Additional hours are dependent on hours being available. A reduction of shifts is dependent upon some being willing to pick up the shifts.

Health Law Concerns:

- *Bandanas (head covering) must be worn in the kitchen at all times. The hairline at the forehead in particular must be covered. Long hair should be tied back.*

- *The middle sink of the second set is the designated hand sink and should be clear of pots at all times.*

- *Food must not be stored or placed on the floor.*
- *Keep your hands and work space clean.*

Meetings: There are periodic cook meetings. Your attendance is desired and sometimes mandatory.

And Finally: During slow times, wash pots, fill spices, tidy up, wipe surfaces, throw out trash, help another cook, help a disher, organize the walk-in – there is a lot to do.

In North Carolina, every restaurant is inspected by the county Health Department. They are required to inspect every commercial kitchen at least once every three months. The inspector arrives with a thermometer to check that cold things are cold and hot things are hot; that food is properly stored (not on the floor). He (it was always a man) watches how cooks are handling the food and at the end gives the establishment a grade. Every restaurant wants to be given an A. We did not always get an A. You could request a re-inspection if you got a poor grade.

When we started, all staff had to have a health card as a condition of employment. This meant that prospective staff had to be tested for Tuberculosis at the Health Department If you tested positive you couldn't work; if you tested negative they gave you a health card which was good for one year. I'm not sure when this practice was phased out, but it is no longer deemed necessary.

Going around with the health inspector was an unwanted task. There were some that were all business, which was preferable to those who told you all kinds of things about themselves that you didn't necessarily want to know. We had one who every time wanted to tell me about his various ailments or his daughter's achievements as a model. Everyone on staff would come to recognize the health man, and we in the kitchen would get a heads-up of several minutes to prepare ourselves.

The early days were chaotic until we settled into or found routines. Initially, we had broad categories: Front or Back; Lunch, Dinner or Late Night; Weekday or Weekend. The front was broken down into waits, cashiers, bars, and bussers. The back: dishers and clean-up, bakers, short orders, cooks, and preps. There were intricacies to be worked out. Who prepared the salad greens? Who made the soups? The salad dressings? The sauces? It was a puzzle to solve. Scheduling took a bit of finesse. Initially Elmer, Mary, and I showed up every day and worked all day. Slowly we got our days off. My first days off were Thursdays and Fridays. But those were only promises and could not be counted on entirely.

Whenever possible, we really did do things ourselves. We made our own yogurt, peeled and chopped our own garlic and ginger. That may not sound like such a big deal, but we had a soup that called for 30 heads of garlic. Now, you can just buy minced garlic or pureed ginger preserved with olive oil in a jar.

Yogurt-making was the task of the late night cook. It was always a hold-your-breath kind of moment when you placed it in the oven to "yog" overnight, wishing, hoping, and willing that it would be yogurt by the time the morning baker took it out. The pilot light of our gas oven provided the low heat – key to turning the milk and starter into yogurt. Typically we would make six 8-cup containers. We needed the yogurt for all the smoothies and Garden of Eden fruit salads. We never achieved a 100% success rate in this endeavor. Maybe not even a 75% success rate. No one was a star yogurt maker.

There was a soundtrack for the kitchen and a soundtrack for the front. For the front we had some definite favorites that eventually turned into if I hear that again my ears are going to explode. We played cassette tapes: commercial tapes and compilation tapes the staff made and brought in. Some of the memorable ones were: the soundtrack from the Robert Altman movie *Nashville* (right now I'm singing "Keep A Goin"); Chris Williamson's album *The Changer and the Changed*, especially "The Song of the Soul" with the words: *Open my eyes that I may see / glimpse of truth thou hast for me / Open my heart, illumine me / Spirit Divine;* Emmylou Harris' *Roses in the Snow;* Bruce Cockburn's *Dancing in the Dragon's Jaws* with the song "Wondering Where the Lions Are;" and Prince's *Purple Rain.* The kitchen was generally quiet when the bakers worked. The day stove and short order brought in the music during the prep time. Music with a beat like Paul Simon's *Graceland* and lots of Reggae.

There was a great deal of conviviality during the time before we were open and then between service hours of lunch and dinner and then after dinner. That was the time for laughter and sharing what was going on in our lives, troubles or joys with relationships. During service hours the atmosphere changed to one of attention to the tasks at hand whatever they might be. At best, we became a single organism – all of us a cog in the wheel that kept turning. A giant cycle of seating customers, taking orders, cooking or assembling the items, serving the food and beverages, bussing the tables, washing the dishes, re-placing the now-clean plates and glassware, making coffee, and cashing the tickets out. It took a real singleness of purpose in which everyone had a needed role to perform. Following the shift we shared a sense of accomplishment and celebration.

Of course, it was not like that all the time. Things could get and did get tense between the front and kitchen staff. It took some effort to keep the philosophy of we're-all-in-this-together going. Sometimes in the heat of the moment things would fly apart. These notes came from the 1984-1987 years, but really, they would have been relevant on any given day or year.

It has come to my attention that there have been some recent problems
between waits and cooks regarding the questionable quality of a food item.
This issue arises every once in a while so I want to generalize my comments to
all the cooks. Basically, it comes down to this: if a wait is uncomfortable
serving an item and requests that it be done over – do it.

The reasoning behind this is as follows: The wait sees the finished product a lot
and knows what an average, superior, or inferior item looks like. The wait is
the one actually presenting it to the customer and will receive the complaint
either verbally or in the form of a bad tip. That bad tip is shared with the
cooks, making it everyone's best interest to provide excellent products all the
time. It is not a personal insult. It took some courage on the wait's part to
voice the request. Please recognize the legitimate part the wait plays in
controlling quality.   MR

And another one:

And now, a sermon: If you are involved in a situation where a wait has
misunderstood a customer order, miscommunicated an order, or made some
other kind of error resulting in an incomplete or wrong order, please move
your body in haste to correct the problem. Immediately, not in a few minutes,
or when it's convenient . . .

The waits are working very hard to present our / your food to its best
advantage and we need to support them / make them look good, as well.

Fixing / repairing orders whosever mistake it is, ours or someone else's, should
be a priority. Also, it would be nice to verbally assure them that you are
jumping on that order. Doing it in silence can be disconcerting for the wait.

End of sermon.

When we started out, all shifts, whether front, back, wait, cook, dishwasher were paid at the same rate: $2 per hour. Minimum wage was $1.65 at the time. Tips were pooled and distributed based on everyone's hours worked. Payroll and tips were paid on alternating weeks so each week everyone got some kind of pay. We owners shared in the tips for the shifts we worked. The staff took care of tip distribution. They had their own bank account and treasurer. I think David Beaudin held this position longer than anyone.

Former staffer Barry Jacobs reflected on how the tip-sharing allowed for a noncompetitive camaraderie among the front staff. There were customers who were known for tipping well and those known for tipping poorly. Since all shared the tips, you did not have to worry about having the poor tipper in your section or resent the fact that the good tipper was being seated in someone else's. In addition, since tips were shared by all the staff, there was no financial disincentive to being trained for other positions.

This continued for many years until the time of either the expansion (1984) or the beginning of Seventh Street (1986), I can't remember which. We were advised by our attorney that, technically, this could be considered coercion: if a tip was given to a wait staff person, the wait was obligated to turn it over to the Crisp Green account. This was maybe borderline illegal, even though the staff, as a whole, was highly in favor of pooling the tips. Losing this arrangement, which was one of the cornerstones of the collective framework of the restaurant, hurt all our hearts. I hated to see this one-for-all-and-all-for-one spirit go.

The work of the restaurant was heavily tilted towards the weekends (Friday night through Sunday night), which required heavier staffing because they were our busiest shifts. It was expected that everyone was going to be scheduled for weekend work. To ease the burden, we came up with a weekend-on and a weekend-off schedule. So you might be scheduled every weekend day or night on weeks 1 & 3, but no weekend shifts on weeks 2 & 4. This worked very well for everyone until we found out that it violated overtime regulations. Since we paid every two weeks, I was not counting overtime until 80 hours were logged. I didn't realize that overtime was computed based on the weekly hours worked. Once enlightened of this labor law, we knew that we could not afford the overtime this system generated and had to forego this nifty set-up.

In the early years, we would look at the big picture and evaluate what money we had accumulated during the year and cut annual bonus checks to the staff based on hours worked. My calendars make note of me working on bonus checks in years 1978 and 1979. Sadly, we did not remain profitable or profitable enough and this practice fell by the wayside.

All Those Co Words: What Do They Mean?

COLLABORATIVE: produced or conducted by two or more parties working together; working together toward a common end.

COLLECTIVE: a group of people acting together.

COMMUNE: a group of people living together and sharing possessions and responsibilities.

COMMUNITY: a group of people living in the same place or having a particular characteristic in common; a feeling of fellowship with others, as a result of sharing common attitudes, interests, and goals.

COMPANY: a commercial business; the fact or condition of being with another or others, especially in a way that provides friendship and enjoyment.

COOPERATIVE: involving mutual assistance in working toward a common goal; a farm, business, or other organization which is owned and run jointly by its members, who share the profits or benefits; a people-centered enterprise owned, controlled and run by and for the members to realize their common economic, social, and cultural needs and aspirations.

CORPORATION: a company or group of people authorized to act as a single entity (legally a person) and recognized as such in law.

In 1973 politics were central, and those we hired were activists and politically minded: Duke graduates who cut their teeth on protests. I think Elmer, Mary, and I thought we would all, the restaurant as a whole, be engaged in a common struggle against society's outside forces; we would be an example of progressive policies in a broken world. We didn't foresee that the three of us would come to represent, to the staff, those very same outside forces. Somethyme would be, in essence, a microcosm of society: the good and the bad, those seen and those unseen, those with power and those without. The three of us were put into the same camp of those we thought we were struggling against. This was shocking to us.

I've been thinking about this quite a bit in my looking back. Why did we become a place of such unrest? One conclusion is that we didn't realize, when we first became partners, that even though the three of us had agreed in principle to make decisions by consensus, the strength of those convictions was unevenly shared. How could we have known? Our brief initial meeting at The Ivy Room was not enough to enlighten us to the differences we would have in attitude. We shook hands and raised a glass to consensus and quickly drank it down.

Of the three, it was Elmer who brought the politics, the ethics of consensus, the idea of mission to the fore as a condition, or guiding principle, of the restaurant. For him, consensus was a pillar of our business model, a marker of our identity. For me, a business run on consensus was a natural extension of my choosing to live in community. I would not have insisted on it, would not have suggested it, had he not, but I willingly concurred. Mary, in all fairness, mostly wanted a restaurant. As long as the decisions were ones that she agreed with, she would go along. It would become clear that she was far more interested in control than in shared decision-making, even within the partnership.

But perhaps most fatally, we were not entirely honest with ourselves about our own feelings of attachment to the restaurant. Before we opened, we held dual and competing understandings of both the restaurant and ourselves. Publicly, we espoused the conviction that Somethyme would be run collectively. Decision-making shared.

Though the jobs might differ, each job and each person had value and the tenet of equality would reign supreme. We anticipated a grass roots, not top-down, management structure. We believed in this structure; it was not a spin or sham. But all along, deep within, unacknowledged and unspoken, we knew ourselves to be its founders. We were the only check signers.

Of interest to me now, and in support of the above statement, is the fact that once Elmer, Mary, and I became engaged in creating the restaurant together, we did not look for additional partners. Although many people worked side by side with us, we did not extend to them an offer of partnership. I think the three of us felt like we were a unit that was whole in and of itself. For us, there *was* a distinction between us and them. It was not a distinction that was overly important, but it was there.

This may be a little wacky, but I believe that words carry meaning and are imbued with power. So I'm looking at the name we chose for the restaurant: Somethyme. Maybe the ambiguity inherent in our name presaged an unconscious and subliminal invitation to questioning and the testing of boundaries. "Some thyme" or "some time" is an answer to the question: "How much?" Or "When?" But it is not a definitive answer. There is room for interpretation. Our name was infused with double meaning; it was nuanced; it had a shape-shifting quality. Somethyme took on, or had from the beginning, those same nebulous qualities.

Once we opened, we learned it was one thing to have an intellectual affinity for sharing responsibility, it was quite another to thread that needle when actual disagreements and problems tested our principles. When we said the restaurant would be run collectively, did that mean that everyone had to agree on the choice of tablecloth fabric or approve of every beer on the drink menu? Did consensus include the voices of both full-time and part-time staffers? What decisions did the owners have responsibility for solely, and what ones could the staff make or share? Did the voice of someone who was just hired carry the same weight as one who had been there from the beginning? Was a person's ability, skill, or job preference a counter-argument against the call for cross-training or job rotation?

The growing expectations of the staff, that we ourselves had created, began to be in conflict with our own sense of proprietorship, let alone efficiency. This divide in perspective, this crack in the veneer became apparent quite quickly. Elmer, Mary, and I began to understand that our sense of entitlement that came with the founding and ownership of Somethyme was not one that the staff held or wanted even to acknowledge. Some thought that there would be no difference between us once our initial investment had been recouped. They referred to us as managers, not owners. They did not want to settle for our version of collective; they envisioned a more expansive model.

By spring of 1974, six months in, these widening divisions led to the creation of position papers. First came our owner statement, followed by one from the staff. When I read these epistles now, my eyes glaze over. There are commonalities between the two, principally that both posited a workplace where the dignity and worthiness of all was of paramount importance. Our statement was measured and cautious in its rhetoric. It was a statement of what was: this partnership of three, this restaurant which served food, this organization which supported progressive thought and the arts. The staff's statement, on the other hand, had a visionary and aspirational feel. The notion of the freedom of expression, the potential of each staff person, the promotion of broad-based "experimentation with food, music, ambiance, and service" as well as a stated willingness to "risk the fate of the restaurant."

The presenting and overriding issue was always some variation of the question: What was Somethyme? Or, Who was Somethyme? Was

Somethyme a community or a business, a partnership or the restaurant, a thou or an it?

Somethyme became the stage for debate about what it meant to be an owner, a worker, a person. We deliberated over the ethics of business. What was profit? What was to be done with profit? What was fair? Was fairness equally fair or was there a scale of fairness? Was one kind of work inherently harder and thus more deserving of higher pay than another? Those discussions were fierce and uncomfortable.

Because of the ideals we shared in common and the belief in the spirit of consensus, we convened meeting after meeting to discuss how to put some meat on those co-bones. In the five months prior to the published position papers, between December 1973 and April 1974, we had 19 various kinds of meetings with the staff: every-other-week general staff meetings, monthly cook meetings, wine tastings, retreats, entertainment meetings, and wage meetings in addition to our own, what we called MEM, weekly meetings. Despite all these meetings with the goal of trying to become of one mind, by spring the lines of dissent and opposition were sharply drawn and produced the following statements.

THE PARTNERS STATEMENT: *SOMETHYME JULY 1973 - APRIL 1974*

Somethyme was conceived in July 1973 when Mary Bacon, Elmer Hall, and Mary Rocap committed ourselves to a collective effort to create a new kind of restaurant that would in some sense carry on the traditions established by Nona McKee and the Bluebird and in other ways offer new and different services to the community. Each of us had fantasized about starting a restaurant but all of us were committed for personal, political, and economic reasons to a collective effort rather than a one-person project. When financial difficulties forced the Bluebird to close in May, the opportunity to try to incarnate our fantasies presented itself. During June, we found each other and decided that our separate visions could intertwine and give each the strength and potential for reality that none had alone. What emerged was a composite hope for Somethyme to which each of us contributed and which all of us affirm.

We hoped to create an excellent natural foods restaurant for all the people of Durham. The selection, preparation, and serving of healthy and tasty food would witness to our own vision of a new harmony with Nature and the Universe and more importantly within ourselves. We know that we are what we eat and we want to refine and simplify our tastes accordingly.

We hoped to create an alternative work-place for ourselves and others. We wanted to create a small business in which people, service, and principles were the clear priorities. We wanted to create structures for work where human creativity and individuality as well as community would occur, a place where we could make a living while exploring work as an experience of liberation and fulfillment.

We hoped to create an institution that would support movements for social change and progressive community groups. This has meant institutionally boycotting non-United Farm Worker Organizing Committee lettuce, Gallo and Portuguese wines. It has meant providing an alternative place of music, poetry, drama, discussions, and politics in Durham. We wanted Somethyme to be a home for progressive people and events.

Two entities emerged from our vision during the next three months, the Somethyme Partnership and the Restaurant itself. The Partnership was created in September as the restaurant was being constructed. It is a legal body of the three founders which has final legal and economic responsibility for the operations of Somethyme Restaurant. The Partnership is a legal collective, all decisions are made by consensus, all responsibilities are equally shared. Membership in the Partnership was defined by initial investment and commitment to work full-time in the restaurant. The Partnership can be expanded to include new members. The Partnership has the responsibility of making policy and decisions regarding the restaurant staff, finances, and relation to various outside agencies and institutions (police, ABC, banks, IRS, etc.)

The role of the general restaurant staff meeting is still growing. At present the staff does assume responsibility for implementing the salary plan approved by the work committee. This involves a commitment to sharing equally tips and that portion allocated for salaries for the general income of the restaurant. The staff also agreed to begin implementing a system of regular job rotation.

Note: For the record, I had never thought of opening a restaurant, but was quite agreeable to try.

This was followed by a staff response dated June 3, 1974:

THE STAFF'S STATEMENT: *A WORD TO THE FOLKS AT SOMETHYME*

We propose to the people of SomeThyme a vision of a further stage in our growth together. We see that the first months of the restaurant have been devoted to assuring its safe continuation. Until now most of our energy has been focused on structural and operational problems. But we have neglected other aspects of what we are about.

We are persons first. And we are persons who are working together towards freedom from the emotional and economic possessiveness and domination by which institutions consume us. In the case of SomeThyme, we see this freedom as being constructed and maintained through the exercise of personal responsibility:

- *The responsibility of each person, to his or her own self, through holding to one's vision of how things should be;*

- *The responsibility of each person here to every other person, through seeking honesty and openness in relationships;*

- *And the responsibility of us all to all persons everywhere, through bearing witness to the truths we jointly hold, through social action in the service of those truths, and through struggling together to make our* own workplace an example of how individuals can work together while yet holding to their integrities within a net of responsible relationships.

A workplace employing members of the loose human web we call our community should be a place where the best values arising from our experience find expression and shape our work and personal relationships. Among these values we believe the following ones are primary:

- First, our workplace ought to foster the richest possible development of personal initiative, and thus should promote the sort of creativity and experimentation with food, service, and entertainment which build the restaurant into a vital, humane, self-consciously growing place promoting the values we jointly hold.

- Second, our workplace ought to foster a genuine equality, a radical democracy, which begins among the staff at large, advances to include the relations between staff and managers, and ends by including all people who touch our life together, not only our customers and friends, but also the salespeople, government officials, and neighbor folks who relate to our scene.

- Third, we believe that our workplace must become a publicly visible, articulate institution, having a vital life of its own, willing to extend a friendly hand to everyone who approaches, us, but also asserting our own values clearly and publicly, although that may sometimes mean risking even the fate of the restaurant.

- Fourth, we believe that central to our achieving these ends is the constant watchfulness by which the influence of money and arbitrary power over our working life can be rooted out, for which reason, we believe that the restaurant as an institution ought to work toward the fullest possible sharing of information about its finances, that the people working together here ought to seek to bring about a radical democracy in financial as well as personal ways, and that ultimately *we believe the entire staff of the restaurant should be intimately involved in reflecting about and deciding substantial issues regarding finances.*

Finally, we wish to say openly that we see ourselves as being in the midst of a process instead of being in a place of completed clarity. We believe that many of our problems in being together have come directly from roles which persons willingly or unwillingly bear because of their duties or because of the difficulty we all have in learning to live outside of the roles we are tempted to take up. Thus, we see ourselves as engaged in a joint struggle, seeking insight into the direction to travel, the values to assert, the goals to seek, but especially the style of human relationship which ought to undergird our work together.

Signers: Jay A. Franklin, Pat McNellis, Aden Field, Lucy Wagner, Martha Maiden, Tom Campbell, Barry Jacobs, Martha R. Hankin, Honorah Domizio, Kent Phelps, John Havran, cyn croxton, Libby McKeithen

Note also the spelling of the restaurant: SomeThyme. We would toggle back and forth between spelling with and without the capital "T" throughout the years.

In hindsight now, I am cognizant of the irony that "co" means "with." Be it collective, company, community, colleagues – it means to be together, with, or not separate from; to be conjoint or combined. I think in all our discussions, arguments, and struggles, we missed something: we were, with each other, doing this restaurant thing for better or worse. We were all engaged in the endeavor – maybe from different perspectives, on different sides – but we were together sharing the tasks, functioning as a restaurant. Maybe there was no answer to the question of who or what Somethyme was. Maybe there was only the being of Somethyme in the time that we shared. Maybe we were our own category, not this, not that, resembling something but not quite a mirror image. The apostle Paul talks about working out your salvation with fear and trembling. That's what we were doing: seeking the holy grail of power-sharing with a goodly amount of raised voices and shaking of fists as well as kumbaya-love and group hugs. We were working out the problems of the world within the confines of 1104 Broad Street. That work was hard. We were more together than apart. Being *with* one another in the endeavor of the restaurant had value and that value was lasting.

When I look at the names of those who signed the position paper now, I am flooded with memories and the realization that we were family, albeit one that was complicated and with issues. In spite of the things (politics) that pulled us apart, there were things (relationships) that bound us together.

I read the name Martha Hankin and I see the Martha who lived right up the street from the restaurant. She was a pie maker, especially good at apple pie. She and I spent many-a-morning together when she'd be making pies and I'd be making bread. Her (then) husband Raoul walked to the restaurant to borrow our scales when their daughter Raven was born; they needed to check her birth weight.

Martha Maiden would go on to buy into the restaurant as a partner and become a life-long friend. She could do everything in the front of the house and everything in the back and do it all well. She cooked, waited, tended bar. I remember thinking I laughed the most and the hardest when I was out and about with her. She came from Memphis, Tennessee to Duke and was one class ahead of me. She had worked at the Bluebird and was a friend of Robin Moran. Robin asked her to help with some of the carpentry before we opened; the two of them built the cashier station. She began working at Somethyme from the get-go.

Martha Maiden; photo by Wicca Paull

Barry Jacobs was also one year ahead of me at Duke. He and Libby McKeithen were living in Rougemont at the time and trying to farm. They grew green beans and had a cow named Bessie. I used to trade them bread for milk. In his heart he was always a writer. Of the initial staff (aside from Martha Maiden), Barry stayed at Somethyme the longest, almost four years. His easy smile, humble attire, and soft-spoken voice belied a tenacity for confronting authority and testing limits. He was all about keeping things real and keeping them on the table. After he left the restaurant he became a freelance writer, writing for local and national papers including *The New York Times* and

Raleigh's *News & Observer*, as well as publishing several books about sports. In addition, he entered politics and held the elected position of County Commissioner for Orange County for twenty years and was its Chair for many of them. He made significant contributions to Orange County, one issue at a time.

Barry Jacobs; photo by Wicca Paull

In short, our lives were intertwined. Both sides felt the disappointment and defeat of not getting along, not getting it right. When I visited Barry on his front porch on a beautiful crisp fall afternoon, he spoke to me of the "violation of the communal spirit" the staff would feel when Elmer, Mary, and I would make what was seen as an arbitrary decision. These failures and bruisings led to attrition of staff and attrition of owners. The issues, unresolved, continued to fester under and above the surface for years. Nevertheless, for myself, the reality of the restaurant, overlaid upon the vision of what might have been or might still be possible, created a depth of experience unmatched by any I have known.

Expanding the Partnership

Somehow, in spite of ourselves, we got through one year. We celebrated this accomplishment on October 17, 1974, and would go on to celebrate every anniversary of Somethyme. We generally followed the tradition set by our first year's party: a shared meal and then a blow-out party with live music and dancing accompanied by a couple kegs of beer and jugs of wine. Here is what I wrote to my folks about our first celebration:

We had our 1st anniversary celebration last night at the restaurant. We are one year old. We closed at 5:00 and had a staff and friends/family pot luck dinner and then partied all night long. We had a band doing rock & roll and we took all the chairs and tables out and had a fine dance floor. Everyone was happily wasted with the beer, wine, music and good feelings – it's weird to think about one whole year – doesn't seem possible.

From an earlier letter to my folks postmarked September 29, 1974, two weeks shy of our first anniversary, I wrote that we were actively thinking about expanding our partnership.

We're working on a new menu now. Business is better than ever but expenses are higher than ever too. Are thinking about expanding the partnership to some of the people currently on the staff. Aden [Field], Martha Maiden, Martha Hankin, Biff Maier are the people who are the possibilities. At least they are giving it some thought and so are we. But nothing definite yet on either side.

Seven months later, on my 1975 calendar, on April 11, I noted that both Robin Moran and Martha Maiden were interested in becoming partners. As it turned out, in September of 1975, a full year after the first mention of consideration, Martha Maiden did become a partner. Mary, Elmer, and I celebrated this as a great philosophical victory, proof that we were not just about wanting to keep all the control to ourselves – that we were, in fact, open to sharing our vision and our very ownership of Somethyme with others.

So while we had proved that we could share the ownership, we had, a little earlier (late 1974 or early 1975), also demonstrated that the partnership trumped the restaurant as an entity. We began claiming an owner's right to be paid a higher salary. Mary began pushing for a salary of $10,000 per year. Elmer must have agreed. I think this discussion may have occurred after our initial investment had been recouped and they felt like the restaurant could now afford it. This translated as $4.80 per hour, more than twice the initial rate we had paid the staff as well as ourselves. We discussed this change with our attorney, Jim Keenan, in his downtown office. I was not convinced it was the right thing to do and remember being so upset that I got up, left the office, and walked the several miles home, fuming. I eventually came around, or gave in, because I can see from my Social Security wage statements that my yearly income rose to $10,000 starting in 1975. As I think about this now I realize that I, unlike Elmer or Mary, was making more money at Somethyme than I had ever made before. This was my first full-time job; I might have felt that I didn't need more: the money I made matched my needs. In contrast, I think they were ready to make more, had been accustomed to making more, and felt like they had waited long enough. That said, one of Mary's consistent complaints about me over the years was that I didn't like money enough.

Looking back, the addition of Martha may have shifted the dynamics of our little partnership or may have confirmed some shifts of dynamics already present. Despite our positive impressions and trust in Martha, within a month I was debating cutting back my hours (which I did) and considering opening up a bakery (which I did not do) and within six months Elmer left for Hot Springs, a little town in the North Carolina mountains. Initially he took a sabbatical, but then he decided to make the move permanent. He sold his Durham home and purchased an inn: Sunnybank. This inn, just off the Appalachian Trail, may have been closer to his dream of food, community, and hospitality than the restaurant would ever be. Forty-plus years later, he is still the innkeeper.

I think it is important to note that it is only after Elmer left, in the spring of 1976, that Mary, Martha, and I began talks with our new attorney, Jean Wilson, about turning Somethyme from a partnership to a corporation as a way of including others in the ownership. I don't know how conscious we were that Elmer's departure left us bereft of the visionary and primary articulator of our mission. What I do recognize now is that we lost his strong voice and conviction, even if that conviction may have tempered with time.

Beyond tax considerations and ownership liability, we discussed how to codify the process of buying shares, be it a significant portion, like Martha had done to become an equal owner, or small amounts that the staff might purchase. We read the book *Small is Beautiful: A Study of Economics As If People Mattered*, a collection of essays published in 1973 by German-born British economist E.F. Schumacher. We considered by-laws. But the more time we spent on it, the more complicated the idea of stock ownership became. What impact would shareholders with unequal financial investment have on our operations? What if we ended up with lots of shareholders? Could we choose who could be a shareholder or could anyone with the cash buy in? How would that change the dynamics of running the business? We spent months wrangling over this, but finally Jean named our unease and advised against multiple shareholders. We decided not to move ahead with the concept of expanded shareholders/owners, but did change our legal entity from a partnership to a corporation.

In retrospect, I see us repeating the earlier pattern: creating an expectation that we were unable or unwilling to deliver. Although we felt we had made the correct decision for ourselves as owners of

Somethyme, we knew it was going to be hard to go back to the staff saying we had rejected the idea of creating shares of the restaurant they could purchase. We knew there would be repercussions. Recently, Martha wrote to me: *I remembered that I was the one selected, and agreed I was the right owner, to tell the staff what we had done. I had trouble sleeping the night before, and had to really be brave in a way I had never been before.*

I can affirm that, of the three of us, Martha *was* the best one to announce the decision; the *only* one with the level-headedness and fortitude to deliver such a statement. She was strong, articulate, and well-respected. I was likely to implode in this type of pressured setting, and Mary likely to explode.

From the staff point of view, the announcement was a complete reversal of what we had said we were working on (opening up the partnership) and was met with anger, accusations of betrayal, general unrest and upheaval. My calendar lists "talk, talk, talk" as staff members sought me out individually to vent their displeasure. The staff coalesced and countered with the formation of a loosely structured union they called The Workers Association. From October 18 (the day after our 3rd anniversary) through December 7, my calendar lists weekly "Negotiating Committee" meetings.

These negotiations included The Workers Association proposals for changes in the Somethyme by-laws. Under the heading Finance Committee they proposed: *The operations of the Finance Committee will guarantee that fiscal decisions be made in democratic fashion. Through their representative on the Committee, all employees – the source of the Corporations' profits – will be given a voice in the allocation of those monies.*

And: *The fiscal affairs of the restaurant shall be supervised by a Finance Committee comprised of the Corporation Treasurer, one manager, one union representative, and one representative of the staff-at-large. Its decisions shall be made by consensus.*

And: *Proposed expenditures in excess of $200 shall be made only with the approval of the Committee, which shall meet as often as exigencies warrant and no less frequently than once a month. Smaller expenditures, some of which must necessarily be made on short notice, periodically will be reviewed by the Finance Committee.*

I found myself in an increasingly untenable place psychologically. My reaction to conflict is basically to go silent and feel terrible. There were a lot of people angry at the direction the restaurant had taken and energized in their response, which I internalized, so I was pretty miserable most of the time. One small but symbolic example I recall is from that December: I was a troubadour at St. Philip's Episcopal Church's annual Madrigal Dinner, going from table to table singing while people ate their roast beef and drank their wassail. Someone asked me to sing "There once was a union maid." All the enjoyment of the evening immediately drained away and my heart was no longer in the singing.

I remained in agreement with the decision we had made but I wasn't thick-skinned enough to work in the negatively charged atmosphere the decision had created. The uncomfortable conditions were exacerbated by complications of my own making, which further muddied the water. I was swimming in my own version of a thick psychic stew.

By 1976 I had moved out of Knox Street and gotten married. Oddly enough, both Mary and I married Davids. My David was a maverick. I had never dated in high school and he was my first steady boyfriend in college. But our steady was always a bit on again / off again. We married in June 1975 and bought a little frame house on Huron Street in the Lakewood area. Within a year into our marriage, I had an affair.

David came to view the restaurant with suspicion and jealousy. The combination of my conflicted heart, the damage my infidelity had caused to our marriage, the loyalty I felt to the restaurant, and the extreme dis-ease I was feeling while at work created a powder keg of internal stress. I did not have the strength or fortitude to keep myself together. "Steady on" was not possible. Something had to give. The something that gave was my role as an owner. We signed the by-laws on July 26, 1976, and by mid-December I had sold my shares and was working what I thought would be my "last" shifts. The restaurant gave me a going away party on Sunday, December 19th.

I did this despite the fact that Somethyme was my world. Here was my work, both vocation and avocation. Here were the people with whom I spent the most time and where those times were mostly spent. If asked, I would have been hard-pressed to identify the lines that separated the Somethyme community and the work of the restaurant from my identity. But under duress, I did draw such a line in an effort to resolve the multiple conflicts with which I was faced. Drawing back from involvement, as divestiture of ownership implied, appeased David and eased the strain of the adversarial politics at the restaurant for me. I had taken on the sting of the staff disapproval as if our decision had been a sin I committed (as was my marital unfaithfulness). My penance was to give it up. I thought this would, in their eyes (and David's), absolve me of my guilt. This may have smoothed some rough places, but in hindsight, I would say it cost me dearly. It was the easy way out, based on faulty thinking. I missed an opportunity for personal growth. I might yet have found or built up the courage to ride out the consequences of the decision. I would have benefited from working with Martha as a colleague, and I would not have drifted through the next several years of my life – I would have lived them.

I don't know if Mary and Martha felt betrayed by my selling my shares. I don't remember thinking that I had abandoned them, but I believe now I did. I was still very interested in the doings and goings-on of the restaurant, but I was no longer responsible for them, and had perhaps proved myself not to be a very responsible person.

My 1977 calendar reflects my tentative re-entry back into the business and the continuity with the Somethyme community, my co-workers and friends. I had kept the bookkeeping duties and after a month-long break from shifts was back to subbing in the kitchen. I remained in a sewing circle with Somethymers Rachel Preston and Jane Collins and in a singing circle with Janet Diamond, Jennie Knoop, and Linda Guthrie. I celebrated my birthday along with fellow Capricorns Bev Dawson and Robin Moran, sang at Martha Hankin's wedding, and was part of the crowd who watched the ACC basketball finals at Barry Jacobs' house. All this and more, but with one notable exception: the Negotiating Committee meetings continued without me.

I started therapy. I remained on good terms with Mary and Martha; we got together for meals. The two of them weathered the storm as did the restaurant, but when it emerged on other side it was without any sense of being a collective or striving to be one.

I recognize the incorporation and the reaction to it as a turning point, a point of no return. Something in the spirit of Somethyme died then. Although the business still had many good years, the conflict it created had taken its toll. In the end, I think I can say, no one came out a winner; everybody lost something. The dream died. Over time, the parties got tired of the struggle and gave up. The Negotiating Committee disbanded. Things finally had been argued to death.

All of this is a deeply specific history. A unique story. Told simply, you could say: We tried something new; it didn't work out. But as it was at our beginning, the closing of this chapter can also be seen as being influenced by the times in which we lived.

The years between 1964 and 1972 are now classified as Counter Culture (although I think the South was somewhat behind this trend). This time period is characterized by an awareness of the fragility of the environment, a new-found interest in organic food and the sustainability of food production, an exploration of lifestyle options, a rejection of fashion constraints, an explosion of music in varying genres, the experimentation with hallucinogenic drugs, and a demand for openness and transparency of information, from the government on down. The protest movements of the sixties and early seventies had come and gone and had actually brought about significant accomplishments. The Vietnam War had been brought to an end. Nixon had been exposed by the Watergate scandal and was gone. Roe vs. Wade brought about access to safe and legal abortion. Earth Day was established. By 1976, the Counter Culture was becoming less and less counter and more and more mainstream; a hybrid model was emerging.

Put another way, maybe you could say that we, as a generation, grew up. The staff that we started with began getting on with what would become the rest of their lives. They moved away, left for graduate school, began their own businesses or found work closer to their own interests; they married and had children. Or, looking for an economic clue, you might say that the economics of stagflation and then inflation were not as supportive to the ideals of idealist thinking. Just living began to require more attention and energy.

Recently I reread *Dune Messiah*, written by Frank Herbert and published in 1977. I found these sentences pertinent:

Empires do not suffer emptiness of purpose at the time of their creation. It is when they have become established that aims are lost and replaced by vague ritual.

Another literary take on the times is from *Jitterbug Perfume* written by Tom Robbins:

The sixties were special; not only did they differ from the twenties, the fifties, the seventies, etc., they were superior to them. Like the Arthurian years at Camelot, the sixties constituted a breakthrough, a fleeting moment of glory, a time when a significant chunk of humanity briefly realized its moral potential and flirted with its neurological destiny, a collective spiritual awakening that flared brilliantly until the barbaric and mediocre impulses of the species drew tight once more the curtains of darkness.

What cannot be denied is that as Somethyme aged, Somethyme changed. It may not have been that noticeable from the outside. We continued to seek out organic ingredients in our food preparation, exhibit local art on our walls, schedule music for our stage, and host fundraisers for progressive causes – all these went on as before, but our commitment to our initial core beliefs began to ebb, and our attention to mission began to drift. Somethyme began to devolve into a place of owners and workers, as is customarily defined, and yet – and yet – against all odds, somehow we managed to retain a deep residue of cooperation, stubbornly marking Somethyme as a different kind of work place. It was just not as exceptional as we, the owners, or they, the staff, had originally dreamt of.

Post Script: A Reflection on the Robbery: August 10, 1976
August 10 was a short two weeks after the by-laws were signed. I had forgotten that the timing of the robbery was so close to the time of widespread staff discontent.

Three deposit bags hidden in the rice barrel were taken sometime Monday night, August 10, 1976. That would have been the weekend receipts since we were closed on Monday. It was $2,210. I'm not sure why the money wasn't already in the bank. Mary discovered them missing Tuesday morning plus some other oddities: the ventilation fan taken from the men's bathroom and a back window opened from the kitchen, neither of which were very big, not big enough for someone to escape through. It looked like an inside job. Since I had placed one of the bags into the rice barrel, the police wanted to talk to me. In a newspaper report, I was identified as an employee although, at the time, I was an owner. (Even now, this irks me.) I remember they came twice to the restaurant to ask me questions, just as we had opened for lunch when I was working a shift, and I didn't have time to talk to them. The third time they showed up at my house, put me in the back of their police car, took me downtown, and fingerprinted me (!!) as a suspect for the robbery. It didn't take too long to convince them otherwise but it was very unnerving. When they were finished Mary came to the police station to take me home. As I recall, she scolded the officers. In any case, other than me, they had no leads.

Since the police had not proved helpful, we sought the help of a detective agency nearby. Their suggestion was to have every staff person submit to a polygraph test. This seemed extreme and we didn't have the stomach to insist that everyone comply, so we did not take their advice.

We never figured out who robbed us. It was a lot of money. It would have covered payroll. We did routinely hide the money in the rice barrel. That would have been common knowledge amongst the staff.

I'm not sure how many people had keys: bakers, late night cooks, but it would have been a fair number. We tended to trust people. And, I think we were right that it was safer to hide the money than have the cashiers take the money up to the bank at night. In hindsight, I think it very likely the money was taken by a staff person as a kind of rude pay-back. In this light, I see it more like an assault than a robbery.

This was not our only robbery. A potentially more dangerous one happened one night after we were closed. A pair of shotgun toting twins wearing bandanas held us up by gunpoint. One aimed his gun directly at the face of cashier, Cameron Dancy, and demanded money. She calmly placed her hand on the gun barrel, edged it away from her face, and gave them the contents of the register. Someone in the kitchen called the police, who arrived shortly afterwards, and apprehended the two who were still in the neighborhood. We got that money back.

That one was an open and shut case, an exciting story in our annals. The former robbery left unanswered questions and suspicions that continue to nag.

Committees

The committee structure which began in March 1975 continued through the whole life of Somethyme and even into Seventh Street. What initially was a novel way for management and staff to work together became the norm. The Personnel Committee focused on hiring, firing, scheduling and any other personnel problems which arose, and the Finance Committee had an advisory capacity with regard to financial decisions. Staff members of both committees served six-month terms. Additionally, with a three-quarter vote, the staff of the restaurant could reverse the decisions of management and the committees.

Mary, interviewed by *The Sun Magazine* in 1977 stated, "Although these practices and committees were originally created out of idealism, they present problems from the standpoint of efficient restaurant operation." And in fact, the Finance Committee did not have a long lifespan but the Personnel Committee (PC) became a permanent feature of our management structure.

The PC was known for asking "What is your sign?" to new applicants. If you were a Scorpio, there would be a long pause, because we always seemed to have a large contingent of employees who were born under that sign. Martha Maiden, a Scorpio herself, honored them by creating The Scorpio Sandwich. It was the best with bread just out of the oven baked by Helen Hancock (hers was airier than mine). Between the mayonnaise-spread slices were sliced tomatoes, Spike, very thin sliced raw onions, alfalfa sprouts, and shaved parmesan cheese.

Below is the initial organizational statement about the committee structure, how it would function, and how membership was to be chosen. It was drafted for the Finance Committee but would come to apply to the Personnel Committee as well.

A STAFF CHOOSING FOR SOMETHYME; MARCH 13, 1975

At a called staff meeting on Monday, 10 March, the SomeThyme staff then present (about 20 persons) agreed to a plan for sharing certain kinds of decision-making in the restaurant. The managers [Elmer, Mary, and myself] caucused during the meeting and agreed (for the partnership) to these propositions:

That there should be created a committee of 5 members (3 partners and 2 persons chosen from the staff at large) to share in making decisions regarding the financial affairs of the restaurant. It was understood that this committee would work by consensus.

This committee will function for 6 months from the date of its creation. The committee will be regarded as an experiment for these 6 months, and will be subject to review and possible extension at the end of this period.

The partners reserve the right to decide whether the committee's work has been beneficial. The staff, however, will be involved in the process of review.

The staff has agreed to a 3-step method of choosing staff members for this committee.

A nominating list is to be posted on the refrigerator at SomeThyme. Persons may nominate either themselves or another person. (The list will permit people to distinguish the type of nomination.) Please put your nominations on the list by Friday, 21 March.

The choosing is to be done first by secret ballot and second (final decision) by consensus.

Secret ballot. A bunch of envelopes will be provided near the nominating list, as well as a complete list of the current staff. Please write out the 3 names from the list that you would like most to be on the financial committee, in order of preference. (Note: Only 2 persons will be chosen for the committee.) Put your choices in an envelope and put the envelope in the suggestion box. The envelopes will be collected for counting before the staff meeting called for 24 March.

Consensus. A special staff meeting has been called for Monday, 24 March, at 2:00 p.m. The purpose of the meeting is mainly to choose the 2 staff members of the financial committee from the group nominated and preferred by the staff. The choosing is to be done by consensus.

Finally, this special staff meeting is also intended to discuss what second decision-sharing committee should be formed. These possibilities have been discussed:

- A Personnel Committee (hiring and scheduling were mentioned);
- A Menu or style Committee (shaping the ambiance of the restaurant was mentioned);
- A Smoothie Committee (insuring smooth daily operations of the restaurant was mentioned).

The entire staff are urged to show their preference in the choosing of committee members, and to attend the meeting on 24 March, so the importance of this matter and related matters can be shared by all.

Signed: Mary Rocap and Aden Field, for the staff

The elections were serious but also lightly contested as you can see by the following campaign statements, one by Dave Steere (a wait) and the other by John Wilson (a cook), posted for a 1983 PC vacancy. Apparently there was a third person running, but I only have these two letters saved in my scrapbook. I will also mention here how delightful it is to see all of this in the actual hand of each writer. We just don't see each other's writing any more. Dave's is printed in pencil with all caps, John's is in ink and in cursive which is rarely used these days. In some ways these papers attest to the fact that the urgings of the staff in the beginning did make an impact and had a positive influence on the development of our identity or personality. Dave won this vote.

DAVE'S CAMPAIGN STATEMENT

"Hurray! Hurray for Dave Steere!"
– Abraham Lincoln
"That Dave! What a Guy!"
– Chris Williamson

Seriously, though, folks, there are basically two main reasons I am running for P.C. They are:

- *I believe the P.C. is a good thing and anyone who believes that should "put in his/her time" working on it; and*

- *I find that I enjoy working at the restaurant more as I get the opportunity to do different things, to expand and vary my duties, so I actually want to work on the P.C. for my own sake.*

Although I realize the P.C is far from a perfect mechanism to make the restaurant democratic, or fair, or co-operative, whatever, I do think it is an unusual and good way to get management to sit down with a couple of employees on a regular basis and talk over all kinds of stuff that is going on in the restaurant. I can't help but think that this kind of regular dialogue is useful for everyone in understanding each other's point of view, and in just getting ideas from different sources put out and maybe put into action. I think we are lucky to have this regular ongoing "forum," imperfect as it is.

Don't get me wrong, I realize that a lot of what the P.C. does is just a hassle for those doing it – scheduling and running around looking for subs is a far cry from engaging in a "meaningful exchange of ideas" etc. But, as I said, I think anyone who thinks the P.C. is important and useful has to be willing to take on this other stuff kind of as a – dare I say it? – duty, to help keep the P.C. alive and well.

As for part 2 above – I think dealing with a variety of hassles is more interesting than dealing with the same ones over and over, and doing different jobs here makes the overall experience of working here broader, more interesting, and more fun, which is of course what matters.

Lastly, I just want to say that I'm not going to take this election process as a personal thing. If nobody votes for me but my mother, that's Okay, I'll just fire my campaign manager and run again some other time. Besides, I plan to vote for one of the other candidates, so why shouldn't you? They can't help it if they're handicapped.

The important thing is that there be active interest and support for the P.C., and that whoever gets elected brings energy to the job, as I am sure any of the three of us running will do.   -Dave

JOHN'S CAMPAIGN STATEMENT

I have had a lot of experience in restaurants and other areas of the food service business. Besides cooking, I have handled hiring and management of part – time personnel, purchasing, and management of material goods. Although I have had little experience in "front of the house" matters, I feel that I could contribute to any dialogue and learn from the experience.

My experience at Somethyme has been positive in the extreme. I feel that the cooperative atmosphere that the organization has promoted from the beginning is the determining factor in my attitude, and I will do my best to keep this spirit alive. On the other hand, I realize that the restaurant business is the most competitive business in town and if professional standards are not set high and kept high this business can go the way of a lot of other really nice places that for some reason just couldn't go on.

If you choose to put me on the P.C., I will gratefully accept your confidence. If not, I will happily enjoy your camaraderie.   -John Wilson

The Middle Years

Although David and Mary's marriage fell apart and they divorced, their relationship was vital and flexible enough that they entertained the notion of becoming business partners. David decided he didn't want to be a forester. He had been working part-time at Somethyme as a late-night wait and got bitten by the bug. Together they opened Pyewacket on May 17, 1977, with David as majority owner (90%) and Mary as minority (10%). David managed the place and Mary provided the menu and recipes. Somethymer Bev Dawson went with him as his kitchen manager. Pyewacket was the name of a Siamese cat from the movie *Bell, Book, and Candle.* It didn't hurt that Mary loved Siamese cats. I thought of Pyewacket as our cousin. Its first location was in the old Wildflower Kitchen site on Franklin Street, Chapel Hill. Eventually it moved to the corner of Franklin and Roberson, the anchor of a beautiful suite of commercial properties called The Courtyard. It was truly a lovely spot. Tom and I enjoyed going there. I almost always got the spanakopita.

By the time Pyewacket opened, I had increased my hours to half-time at the restaurant and had a side gig of baking from home for Beautiful Day Natural Food Store and the Durham Co-op. David Bacon asked me to bake bread for Pyewacket, which was an honor. I came up with a new recipe which I liked quite a bit: wheat berry. The problem was that it was a heavy bread and always had a hole in the middle. It was a disaster and I couldn't seem to fix it. After about two months I gave up. I don't know why I just didn't come up with another recipe or bake it longer, maybe at a lower temperature.

But, frankly, I was baking "under the table" in our home. I had bought a pizza-style oven and put it in the basement. It was huge. It could hold 16 2# loaves at a time. The temperature was even. I made the dough in the kitchen and then carried the formed loaves downstairs for baking. In an effort to become legitimate, I requested that the Department of Agriculture come and inspect my kitchen so that I could, hopefully, become an honest working woman. They did come but said they would not certify my kitchen. Period. There was nothing I could do to make it work. I never even showed them the oven I was really using. I continued to bake after their visit but slowly pulled out of my baking commitments: first Pyewacket, then the Co-op, and finally Beautiful Day – at which point I picked up hours at the restaurant until I was back to full-time. Ninth Street Bakery bought my oven when they first opened in 1981.

In December 1978 Martha sold her shares and entered graduate school at UNC/Chapel Hill in Astronomy. She had always been interested in the stars and was the restaurant's resident astrologer; she would eventually end up working for NASA. After Martha left, Mary began sprinkling her conversations with talk about selling Somethyme. I realized the restaurant might not always be there and I might should begin to consider a Plan B. I thought maybe nursing might be an option and enrolled at Durham Technical Institute (DTI) in their Practical Nursing Degree Program. Throughout the program I maintained a couple dinner cook shifts and, of course, the bookwork.

The 12-month course was spread over four quarters. It only cost $26 in tuition per quarter plus books and uniforms and such. Even at the time, I considered this price generously affordable and a gift to the community. I loved learning about the body and how it worked, aced all the tests. But when it came to the practical side, and this was Practical Nursing for goodness sake, I was a dolt. I had a hard time with the notion that I had to do real things to real people when I did not, in fact, know how to do them: give a person a shot, take their blood. I couldn't get over that. Despite feeling borderline incompetent, I graduated in December of 1979, got pinned in the pinning ceremony at Duke Chapel, passed the boards, and got certified. I even found employment: the good doctor Curt Eshelman hired me for some part-time work at his Lakewood Family Practice.

Although I was grateful that Curt trusted me, I longed for something I was good at, which was, as far as I could tell, restaurant work, specifically Somethyme Restaurant work. The restaurant was still compelling. I could do any kitchen shift. I could do front work. I enjoyed them all: the cashiering, bussing, and "floating." By January of 1980, I resolutely turned my gaze back to the restaurant and put together a pretty varied schedule: books on Monday, cashiering lunch on Tuesday, ordering on Wednesday, and dinner stove shifts on Thursday and Friday.

In June, I joined the Board of Directors as a non-shareholder. Also on the Board was Duke Divinity School professor Bill Poteat. Bill was the father of a childhood friend of Mary's and a wildly popular professor in the Religion Department. I had taken one of his classes because everyone said it was a must. And it was. It was a distinct honor to serve with him on the Board, the duties of which were simple: have a meal together once a year and talk, briefly, about the restaurant.

In the meanwhile, my marriage was coming apart at the seams. By 1979, David's maverick-ness had turned into full-blown paranoia. I won't go into the details, other than to say that my sandals were never a recording device nor was my necklace a microphone. I became the kitchen manager in August 1981, just in time. By then, it was only a matter of when I would have the wherewithal to leave David. The restaurant became a source of stability, reassurance, and (truly) sanity, and I embraced it fully. Restaurant friends were crucial to my mental health during the final year, months, and days of my marriage. Their support and counsel were soul-saving.

By this time, all ideas of the staff unionizing had dissipated. A fairly predictable pattern of the owners/managers consulting closely with staff via the Personnel Committee (PC) and Kitchen PC (KPC) had become established. It wasn't perfect, but it was sustainable. Things lost their political edge. Conflicts transitioned onto the softball diamond. We entered a phase of playing regular games against Pyewacket, and, later on Wellspring. I kept score; Mary was the cheerleader. It was us vs. them, but now all of Somethyme was in the "us" category.

I left David on November 3, 1981, Mary giving me immediate shelter. Fortunately, within the week I was able to move in with my good friend Karen Sindelar, a Knox Streeter, who was living in Forest Hills. In November of '81, my yet-to-be husband, Tom Prince, was living in St. Petersburg, Florida where he had grown up. Obviously, this is some distance from Durham, but there were two pertinent connections. One was Tom's high school girlfriend Leslie Carter. Leslie had been working at the restaurant since 1977. Her sister Anne and brother Jeff were working for us as well. (I consider them to be one of Somethyme's dynasties. It was at Somethyme that Leslie met her husband, Eben Rawls, and where Eben met his law practice partner, Tony Scheer. Brother Jeff is now a restaurateur himself.)

The second connection was Art Knowles, a St. Pete transplant, who lived in Durham and was dating one of our bakers, Alice. Tom and Art were old friends. While visiting Florida later that month, Alice told Tom that Somethyme was looking for a cook. Now Tom was a cook. He had worked in some very fine establishments in St. Pete and was footloose and fancy-free at the time. With only the prospect of a job at Somethyme, he drove up to Durham in his sky-blue Volkswagen bug.

It was after a breakfast (which included a Bloody Mary or two) that Leslie convinced Tom that "now" would be a great time to check out that job at Somethyme, and it was. It was a Monday, early December; the restaurant was closed and I was doing bookwork. Tom was relaxed and smiling (and if you know him, a smiling Tom is not that common a sight). Being desperate for help, and not altogether unaffected by his smile, I hired him straight away. During those early months of Tom's employment, I was never sure how he liked working in the kitchen – he was always so serious and disgruntled-seeming much of the time. Actually, I was sure he thought I was a Terrible Kitchen Manager, maybe the worst he had ever had. Then one day we were both in the kitchen, me walking in, him walking out, when he said "Just one more thing . . ." My heart dropped, thinking: Now What?. . . "Can I have a hug?" Hmm, OK and so we hugged. At first my head was against his shoulder and face pointed outward, but quite soon I found myself, in spite of myself, turning my face so that it was cradled against him, toward his heart. He felt perfect; I felt at rest. That was in August 1982. In September we started seeing each other, specifically September 10, and that was that.

Six months later, we bought a house on Wilkerson Avenue. On April Fool's Day the following year, he asked me to marry him while he was chopping lettuce on one side of the prep table and I was chopping onions on the other. I wondered whether or not he was kidding but said "OK" just in case. He said "When?" I said "Maybe September."

We did get married in September. We drove to the courthouse in downtown Durham and were married by a judge. Our witnesses were Charlie and Lise, Mary, Helen Griffin, and Linda King – Somethymers one and all. In the earlier years of our marriage we had a hard time remembering our wedding anniversary since the date was never set. The construct we were working under was that we needed to get married sometime within 30 days of the day we had gotten our physicals. But with time, our memory has improved. It was September 14, 1984. Mary gave us a surprise reception back at Anotherthyme with wedding cake and champagne.

At the judge's office getting married; photo by Helen Griffin, 1984

The reception back at Anotherthyme; 1984

Anotherthyme

In 1982, Mary's thoughts about selling the restaurant started to coalesce. She decided to close Somethyme and open another restaurant, Anotherthyme. Since I was now the kitchen manager, I went along with her as she looked at various locations for the new restaurant. We looked pretty seriously at Brightleaf Square in downtown Durham, a former tobacco warehouse, which was just beginning to be renovated for commercial use. Then it came to Mary's attention that the restaurant Maitland's was up for sale. Maitland's was one of a group of restaurants owned by a single family. Their other places included The Top Hat (across the street from Somethyme), Nance's Cafeteria, and Nance's Seafood. But Maitland's, on Gregson Street right around the corner from Brightleaf, was the top of their line. It had a very nice set-up, was cozy and elegant. Mary liked it and bought both the restaurant and the building.

It began to dawn on us that maybe she didn't have to close Somethyme; maybe there could be both a Somethyme and an Anotherthyme. We talked and came to the conclusion that I would stay at Somethyme and hold down the fort, thus allowing Mary the freedom to focus on Anotherthyme. She would still be active in Somethyme's management but most of her time would be spent at Anotherthyme. Anotherthyme opened on May 1, 1982.

Even though, at that point, Mary was the sole owner of Somethyme, Somethyme had, by then, accumulated a lot of baggage. Anotherthyme offered her a fresh start. Here was a restaurant that she could truly call her own, make her own. She had full control over the menu, the policies and procedures, and its operation. There were no committees to confer with, no partners with whom she would need to negotiate. She was able to do it her way, even keeping her beloved German shepherd with her in the office, just off the front seating area.

She would run afoul of the Health Department for this practice, but did not care.

A year following the opening of Anotherthyme, Mary invited me to buy back into Somethyme and worked it out financially for me by raising my salary so I could afford to pay her for the shares. I became a 1/3rd owner. I also worked at Anotherthyme doing their payroll every other week. I did this for a dining credit of $25 per payroll.

When I bought back in, things felt upbeat, as this announcement dated June 11, 1983, attests:

Mary Bacon and I are pleased to announce that I am buying back into the restaurant. I will be a 1/3rd owner with Mary retaining 2/3^{rds} of the shares.

I have to laugh at myself as my relationship continues to change over the years with this restaurant. From being owner to half-time owner to bookkeeper to Board of Directors to cook sub and staff person to kitchen manager and now back to owner. There have been reasons behind all those changes and I regret none of them but people outside and inside the restaurant have had a hard time keeping up with them.

As Somethyme approaches its 10th anniversary I feel like it's time for me to commit more structurally to what I know and recognize to be the work that gives me so much substance. Because I receive so much from Somethyme and it means so much to me I want to contribute my labors with Mary as an affirmation of its past and potential for the future.

Mary wanted this note to convey her happiness over this decision. It has been her desire ever since I sold out 7 years ago.

There will be a staff meeting pretty soon. Mary and I would like to pop some champagne afterwards. Please join us for a toast.

Mary sent me flowers accompanied by this note:

Congratulations, MR. And thank you for your continued love and affection for this great restaurant. Your decision has brought me much joy and hope it will also do that for you – good luck, I love you, MSB June 1983

Since later that year we would be having our 10th anniversary, we decided to make it a big one. We decided to treat it like a Homecoming and made a special effort to invite everyone who had ever worked there.

Dear Somethymers,

As the 10th anniversary of Somethyme approaches on October 17th, Mary Bacon and I decided to try to contact as many as possible of our former staff and invite you to the party.

To date we have had 302 people work for us (Steve Darling the longest at 5 years). I enjoy reviewing the list from time to time and bringing your faces before my mind's eye. The Somethyme staff has always been a varied group of characters, all of whom have left a mark. Geb Adam's painting is still on the men's bathroom wall, the Nancy Dickinson "Memorial Wait Station" still holds water glasses, Peter Marsh's chute still conducts endless trash bags to the dumpster, Jeannie Cheeseman's cheesecakes and bagels are still made every Monday, Biff Maier's bench still surrounds Booth #1, and Robin Moran's touches are everywhere. Thank you all.

Some of the former staff we hear from off and on. Others who are still in the area are connected in new ways: Russell Rigsbee hasn't bussed dishes in years but comes in every morning for a cup of coffee; Aden Field meets accounting clients here for lunch; Rachel Preston grows summer table flowers; I order food from Portia McKnight and Flo Hawley who work at Wellspring Grocery Store; and we buy croissants baked by Libbie Hall from 9th St. Bakery operated by Mo and Michael Mooney. The circle of Somethyme and our connections widens and widens with the years.

We were closed a week in June to (at last) put down a new kitchen floor. Everything had to be removed. When I looked into that empty space, the heart of the restaurant, I was struck by how minute it was. Tiny! And yet it has been the stage of such diverse stories.

It would be nice to gather together for a re-telling of some of them. Think about it. We're going to have a celebration. It would be nice to see you.

The Anniversary Party was a big success. Many former Somethymers showed up or sent cards and letters. Mobile City played and I, as a Mobilette, sang with them. The place was packed. I loved singing and being able to watch everyone having a good time and dancing to our music. The fact that Elmer was there and that the three of us, the original partners, could celebrate ten years of Somethyme was deeply meaningful. Each of us had a feeling of pride and accomplishment, a love for the place and for each other, and a shared joy of experiencing the moment together.

Me, Elmer, and Mary; 1983

Jay Miller, Me, Elmer, Mary, and Lise Uyanik; 1983

Some people I see: Mike Ancel, Biff Maier, Marsha Proctor, Randy Campbell; 1983

More festivities; 1983

A Place To Come To

(FOR SOMETHYME) BY GEORGANN EUBANKS

I think of late afternoon light
Shadows cast long across tables and chairs,
Quiet talk and a woman's voice: music,
A fan stirring overhead.
I sip tea and remember five years
Of friends come and gone through here:
This meeting place, familiar as home.

A thousand meals we have shared:
Fresh, warm bread and honey, butter and cheeses –
Sustenance essential, prepared by a dozen hands
A communion secular but serious – your gift to me.
It is not the exchange of money
That has made you thrive; it is
Something immaterial and as precious as good health.

I can mark my years in this town by menus:
Lunches, talking business over coffee
Dinners of celebration or of loneliness
Late night conversations washed down with wine –
Lifting up my mind's confusions and revelations
Plans and promises made, fulfilled and broken,
All this within your rough-hewn walls and in my memory.

I collect these images
The food of my friendships and folly
And with a magazine tucked under my arm,
The table cleared, dishes returned to kitchen
Where something new is cooking,
I leave, satisfied and grateful for
A place to come to.

The Expansion

Once Anotherthyme opened in 1982, for good or ill, there were now two restaurants located within five miles of each other (and one in the next town) with common dishes on their menus. We had thought the customer base would be strong enough to support both Thymes in Durham and Pyewacket in Chapel Hill. Anotherthyme's location in the downtown district had the potential for drawing in business customers for lunch, and with its lavish bar, offered the possibility of a lively and sophisticated Happy Hour, but it also had the unintended consequence of siphoning off some of our business.

Anotherthyme seating area; photo by the Indy Weekly

Anotherthyme had rich green carpeting, peach painted walls, twinkle lights suspended from the ceilings, and cloth napkins. The bar was stunning. Definitely upscale. With Anotherthyme's opening, Somethyme began to languish on the vine and we began to look at ourselves in a different light. Anotherthyme was elegant and Somethyme looked a bit shabby in comparison. Although Mary had "offered" to hire those who wanted to work at Anotherthyme from Somethyme's ranks, she was choosy. Some were acceptable to her and others were not. This was particularly true of the front staff and fed a growing sense of being less than which we had never considered before.

Somethyme had started out its days being fiercely loved by its founders and staff. Its interior and exterior were marked by the personalities of the creative people who worked there. Our bike rack was an iron bed stand. Our blackboard was decorated every morning by the lunch cashier. The music we played was staff-curated. We had a homemade authentic look. It was a style congruent with our food and we had embraced it for nine years.

Suddenly we didn't feel as proud of ourselves as we once did. We were sisters and as sisters often do, we developed a sibling rivalry. For all the turbulence of the early years resulting from a seeking, earnest, and dedicated staff, the troubles of the latter years were debilitating and damaging, coming from jealousy, competition, and increasing financial insecurity.

In 1984, our 11th year of business, Sanders Florist decided to relocate to the free-standing building next door recently vacated by Reilly Auto. Mary and I talked about the idea of Somethyme expanding into 1102 Broad, of getting a make-over and smoothing out some of our rough edges. Maybe that would put a needed spark into our business. We decided to do this. We took out a $50,000 loan from Central Carolina Bank (CCB) for the renovation; Mary put up her home on Markham as collateral.

To give our expansion a context, between July 1981 and November 1982 the U.S. economy had been in a recession. That may have been part of the reason why business was sluggish. At the time, it was considered the worst economic downturn since the Great Depression. Inflation rates rose during the seventies and into the early eighties, some years (1974, 1979, and 1980) going above 12%. Interest rates went as high as 20%. However, by 1983 the country was starting to come out of it. At the time, the interest rate may have been 12%. We must have seen this frighteningly high rate – by today's standards – as low, or at least lower, than what the rate had been in the recent past.

I remember sitting with Mary in the back staff booth, stressing about the cost of the expansion, and she looked at me and said "We don't have to do this; we can use the money to just freshen up this side." We hadn't started; hadn't done anything we couldn't undo. If I had said out loud the "Let's not" I said to myself, I think Mary would have agreed, but after that conversation we never revisited the matter.

We hired the local legend restaurant architect John Lindsay to design the layout of new space. Knox Streeter Bill Matthews, a skilled carpenter, and his business partner Tim Crowley agreed to do the work. The expansion solved many of our cramped space issues providing much-needed room for kitchen operations and storage, as well as office space. We bought a commercial automated dishwasher and additional refrigeration units. We reorganized the kitchen prep area and production line. We had begun serving mixed drinks several years before, but with the additional front space we put in a full bar with bar stools (and a TV!) and offered an expanded line of liquor, cocktails, and soda drinks (including Coca-Cola). The new side significantly increased our seating capacity. We added chicken to the specials menu and opened for breakfast on weekdays. Besides polishing up the interior space we decided to upgrade the look of the wait staff. No more blue jeans! It was a lot of change. A Lot of Change.

The new side and the frame of the bar with Tim, me, Bill, and Mary; 1984

In hindsight, oh my goodness, so much change. What follows is my attempt to unpack these changes – step back and assess the whys and what-fors that led us to make them because they are pretty different from what came before.

One: We became Somethyme Restaurant & Bar. This was something we had argued we weren't going to be when we first got our beer and wine license back in 1974 and was a huge identity change for us as a restaurant. But it reflected a change in the culture of North Carolina in law and custom. When we opened, mixed drinks were illegal. In 1978, North Carolina ended a ban that had been in effect for 70 years and legalized mixed drinks. True, between 1967 and 1978, the state did allow brown-bagging. Under brown-bagging laws, you could dine at a restaurant, bring with you your own liquor in a bag, order soft drink set-ups, and then mix your drinks at the table. Since we did not sell soft drinks, no one, to my knowledge, ever took advantage of brown-bagging to make themselves a drink at Somethyme. We did not get a mixed drink license when we could have in 1978, but three years later applied for one and on September 22, 1981 began selling mixed drinks and liquor. At that time, we began to stock soft drinks, although they were the natural foods versions of cola, root beer, and ginger ale. It would not be until our expansion that we added Coca-Cola to our beverage line, installing a soda gun in the bar. In our 1973 opening welcome statement, we said *"Some of our foods, such as sugar, cream cheese, coffee, and alcohol are not necessary for a healthy diet; consequently these items are offered as options to our basic menu."* But with our expansion, we invested in and promoted beverages that exemplified a contemporary or cosmopolitan feel rather than a health-oriented one. This was completely contrary to our opening vision. The fact is, I do not remember discussing the ethics of selling liquor with Mary – it did not seem to be a big deal at the time. It was the economics of selling liquor that led the way: there was a good margin (cost vs. selling price) to be made on the sale of alcohol. And then, of course, we weren't teetotalers. We both drank – she more than I, but I did (and do) enjoy a vodka tonic from time to time.

Linda King, Queen of the Bar; photo by Ann Rocap, 1984

Another bar view; photo by Ann Rocap, 1984

Two: We began adding chicken to our offerings. Mary and I and most of the cooks were no longer strict vegetarians. We ate chicken. We ate meat. Mary wanted to stretch her culinary repertoire and we did get organic, free range chicken initially. We thought including chicken would widen our general appeal and strengthen our customer base. Would this have happened if Elmer had still been with us? Probably not. His Sunnybank Inn is still vegetarian after all these years. Interestingly, Anotherthyme remained vegetarian until the early 1990s.

Three: We opened for breakfast. Saturday and Sunday Brunches were our most popular shifts. We consistently served 200 diners at each brunch. We thought opening for breakfast during the week would also be well patronized. Either our menu was too involved or the cooks who worked the shifts weren't up to the task, but we got a reputation for being slow right away, which cut into the clientele who might have come in before going to work. The extension of hours turned out to be a scheduling and administrative burden. One could, if need be, work a double (both the lunch and dinner shift) but working all three was a bridge too far.

Four: We initiated a dress code: no jeans. In the 1970s, the fashion statement was the hippie look: jeans, bandanas, tie-dyes. This totally matched the dress of our staff. It was fashionable in an unfashionable counter-culture way. By the 1980s, the look had moved on to spandex, padded shoulders, permed and big hair. The front staff, led by the cashiers, were for the most part, following the national trend although we did have some die-hard hippies still onboard.

Five: The new space had a different look in and of itself. It was airy and bright due to the natural light streaming in through the side in addition to the front windows. It didn't have the dark and intimate character of the old side. We chose a color scheme to match the feel of the new side inspired by a Navaho blanket Mary had: dusty purple and orange. In the '80s, neon colors were the rage, orchid purple the most popular color of 1984. So while the colors were not as flamboyant as they might have been, they did not harmonize with the warm, rich browns and orange of the old side. Nor did the fixtures and furnishings. Our original tables were wood; the new custom-made tables were topped with orange laminate and bordered with oak strips. The old booths were converted pews or slabs-of-wood benches; the padded cushions of the new booths were made of purple vinyl. The new side was South-Western desert; the old side was Chatham County tobacco barn. They were a world apart.

Six: We hired out the work. True, those we hired were our friends, but they were paid contractors – we didn't have that sizable core of volunteers to do the non-skilled tasks nor did we do that work ourselves. (And how could we, as we were already running a restaurant?) The implementation turned out to be very expensive, exceeding the budget. The $50,000 we borrowed did not cover the cost of the expansion, partly because city codes finally kicked in forcing us to include changes we hadn't anticipated like putting in a back door. The building no longer qualified for a grandfather waiver once we undertook such a major renovation. Although we applied, the bank would not increase the money they loaned us. Reluctantly, Bill and Tim agreed to take their final payments in the form of restaurant meal credits. The plumber was not interested in such a deal, and we had a hard time squeezing out the money to pay him.

As renters of our space, we were on the financial hook for every upgrade within the walls of the building. The owners were responsible for the roof and outside walls. When, early on, we replaced the swamp cooler with an air conditioner, we paid for that. When we upgraded the electrical system, put quarry tile on the kitchen floor, replaced the hood and exhaust system, we paid for that as well. And now, the changes that came with the expansion: the beautiful new bar and the new bathrooms, which are still being used today by the current tenant, were improvements we paid for. All these upgrades were things that stayed with the building – leasehold improvements made using thousands of our own nickels and dimes.

Prior to the expansion we were able to pay our bills every month. I never had to hold my paycheck until there was enough money in the bank to cover it; we had never before bounced checks. Right away, things became difficult. I myself, between August 1984 and January 1985, made three loans to the restaurant totaling $8,500 trying to ease cash flow.

We opened in September. Some of this change, as I have tried to illustrate, was just a sign of the times; some of it was self-inflicted. We had a new space which offered new possibilities and we went with that. We didn't adequately consider the optics and ambiance, the blend of the two sides, the additional work load, the additional staffing. Although the expansion solved some problems, it also brought issues we hadn't considered and challenges we were not ready for.

Our customers did not embrace the new space. They didn't like the airy aesthetic; they didn't like entering from the 1102 door; they would rather sit on the old, more cloistered non-smoking side than the new one (which became the smoking section/side of the restaurant), and they didn't like that we had abandoned our vegetarian and hippie roots. From that time forward, we were playing a defensive game. Even Elmer sent a complaining note saying something to the effect of: "Congratulations. I hear that you are Somethyme in name only – you are now selling blood and coke."

There was an editorial in Duke's *Chronicle* on September 4, 1984 under the title "Polyester: the Epitome of America," which included the following:

It is sad to report that the very heart of Durham's cultural eating establishment has sold out to this very same mindset. Somethyme Restaurant now looks like a Denny's. In contrast to the warm, earthy atmosphere of the old Somethyme, the new addition's stark whiteness seems frigid and sterile. The natural wood paneling of the old has been sacrificed for man-made drywall of the new. Unlike the intimacy of the original dining room, the new one loses all sense of this feeling as it emphasizes Space Age independence. Not only are the tables placed very far apart, but now there is a bar at which an individual may sit in total isolation.

Tom wrote a rebuttal to this article which, as far as I know, was never printed.

[The] article calling Somethyme Restaurant's improvement a sellout and a venture into the world of polyester imitation is bordering on misuse of the press. [The author] ignored a most important point in expressing his or her contempt. Somethyme is a direct link to the food chain. Our purpose is still to provide the community with the realest, freshest, most nutritious, tastiest variety of foods available. We do a good job of it. We buy as much local produce as possible. Many people have learned to bake and cook here. Very few restaurants are organized to cook from scratch. There is no sellout here, only hard work.

Concerning the esthetics of the new side; two of the finest carpenters I've seen made a gigantic effort and orchestrated other tradespeople to create a strong original design. Most of our time and money went into woodwork. How can [the writer] miss the contrasting varieties of wood? Armadillo Restorations treats wood as it should be treated, a precious, natural substance. I couldn't even find pieces big enough to salvage. Tung oil sure makes a nice finish.

[He] seems to equate intimacy with a lack of elbow room. The new space has already kept a few people out of the rain who would have otherwise only had

room on the sidewalk. A little extra space is helpful in avoiding collisions of wait people with trays of food. I disagree with [his] contention that a bar is an isolated place to sit, though we do now have a booth where that is nearly possible.

On the day Tom and I got married, I went into the restaurant and opened the mail to find a vitriolic letter saying how much the writer hated the restaurant now. Among his complaints were items that were simply not true: "You don't even serve brown rice anymore." "I hear you are going to take down the wood siding." I probably shouldn't have gone in, but I was full of anxiety about the restaurant and couldn't keep away. Needless to say, my anxiety was not alleviated.

In order to deflect or answer this widely felt criticism, we came up with a statement which we printed on little tent cards and placed on every table:

Given our history as a mainstay of vegetarian cuisine in the Triangle area, we feel we owe you an explanation. The fact is, we have decided to include poultry among our special dinners from time to time, and we are likely to include one or two of these dishes when we revise our menu at year's end.

For the strict vegetarians among you, this may be disheartening news. We wish to stress, however, that vegetarian dishes still dominate the menu and Somethyme remains committed to the goal of providing a variety of nutritious foods, including all of the whole grains, fresh fruits and garden vegetables that have been our staple for the past twelve years.

The move to poultry is being prompted, in part, by the need to widen our clientele in order to remain competitive in a fast-changing market. We hope therefore, that we can count on your continued patronage.

The Somethyme Management.

POSTSCRIPT ONE: Having a Liquor License came with oversight by the Alcohol Beverage Commission (ABC) and enforcement by the NC Alcohol Law Enforcement (ALE), a division of the NC Department of Public Safety. This was no small matter. Gun toting, seriously unfriendly enforcers would make surprise inspections to make sure we were buying and serving stamped alcohol. Stamped alcohol is alcohol bought from the ABC store using your license number to make the purchase. It is taxed at a higher rate and therefore more expensive than if you were simply buying a bottle for yourself to take home and drink. Once emptied, every bottle had to be broken immediately to prevent someone from refilling it, "passing" it as a stamped bottle.

POSTSCRIPT TWO: It seems odd now to think of smoking sections, let alone smoking in public spaces so accustomed are we to smoke free protections. When we first opened, smoking was allowed everywhere – no such bans were on the books. It wasn't until 2010 that the tobacco state of North Carolina banned smoking in restaurants. California was the first state to do so, in 1995. But restrictions on smoking began showing up in various states in the 1970s.

I don't think we initially had a smoking vs non-smoking section when we first opened, because I remember that we used to put ash trays on all the tables as part of set-up, but soon enough, the back area become the designated smoking section (which included the staff booth). The new side of the restaurant, dominated by the bar, became the smoking side.

Another Ownership Change

Sometime between our wedding on September 14 and November 12, when her name showed up on some Kitchen Meeting notes, Mary decided to sell all but 10% of her shares to Jenny Wears. Jenny was the fiancé of Mary's ex-husband, David Bacon. She had come into an inheritance and was looking for an investment. Her investment translated into 57% of the restaurant. Mary told me of the concluded sale over the course of a dinner we were having together at Anotherthyme. I felt blind-sided and was deeply hurt by this decision. Although one condition of the sale was Jenny's provision that I remain, these negotiations did not include me and in fact occurred behind my back. I understood that Jenny's request that I remain was meant for good, but that did not prevent me from feeling used and taken for granted, as if I were a chess piece being played for another's advantage. I did agree to stay, but not without considerable resentment. Aside from my personal reaction, it felt, business-wise, that Mary was abandoning the restaurant on the heels of a disaster. My relationship with her, which was never entirely even-keeled, immediately took on a new complexity.

Even though I went through these cycles of retreat and re-engagement, it was not because I disliked the work – it was the emotional intensity of the work environment that I had a hard time tolerating. It turns out that I have a low comfort threshold for conflict. In the early years, there were the issues between the owners and the staff. But through it all, there was Mary.

I would be disingenuous about the restaurant if I did not in some way acknowledge Mary's role in creating and maintaining tension within the business. I came to see her as a two-sided coin: one that could flip back and forth without warning. On the one side, generous and warm; on the other, hard-edged and volatile – both tinged with the possibility of manipulation. She was a force of nature more likely bringing her storm than her sunshine. I often felt caught between her actions and the staff upon whom those actions were directed. When the two of us tangled, we never properly sorted the issues out because I frequently kept my resentments to myself. I developed an external self and a hidden self when it came to Mary. I do not want to dwell on this aspect of the restaurant – if you worked there, it is likely that you have a memory of one kind or another of an incident or conversation about or with Mary. These encounters shaped the experience of working at Somethyme, mine included.

The new ownership structure upended the dynamics of the restaurant, turning what had been known (though fraught) into something unknown (and fraught). Jenny was, and is, a gentle person with good intentions. She threw herself into the place; if conditions had not been as dire it might have worked out. She could have been the gracious person she was in the front and brought her good ideas to the kitchen. But at the time, we didn't have that luxury.

Along with Jenny, Jill Cotter entered the picture about this time. Jill had become a kind of unofficial consultant to Mary at Anotherthyme. Although she did not have a restaurant background, she had a kind of business savvy and drive that inspired confidence and Mary began to lean on her for advice. Initially Jill came over to Somethyme, at Mary's request, to see if she could be of any help.

We welcomed her in; she became part of the Somethyme management team along with Jenny. The evidence I have for their joint appearance are those kitchen meeting notes from November 12, 1984. Their initials appear at the bottom: JW, TP, MR, JC [Jenny Wears, Tom Prince, Mary Rocap, Jill Cotter]. Prior to that there is no mention of either one in my journals or kitchen meeting notes.

This is a good time to say something about Tom's involvement with the restaurant. The running of which was something we came to share. I was fortunate that he was both interested and capable. He was versatile in his skills; he was a baker, day or night stove cook, and prep cook. Over time he began to pick up back-of-the-house management duties, beginning with ordering and ending up as kitchen manager. He worked there from December 1981 into June 1986.

Tom; photo by Ann Rocap, 1984

And also something about Lise's expanding role. About the time I bought in, I noted in my journal that my dear friend and singing mate Lise Uyanik Ebel was interested in working at the restaurant. I did a little thinking about it noting that, on the plus side, she liked Somethyme, had management skills to offer, had a good image. But I also worried how working there might affect our friendship. Lise did join the staff in 1983 working as a cashier before becoming a front manager in 1985. Thankfully, she remains one of my closest friends today.

Tom's Kitchen Personnel Committee notes of January 8, 1985 stated this:

A rough start to what seems a promising year. Good life to us all. Jenny Wears has some good seafood ideas. Be on the lookout for stuffed trout; perhaps salmon with cucumber hollandaise, a low calorie broiled scallops, a new salad dressing, a fruit dessert . . . international nights (one per month).

As Tom pointed out, 1985 began rough; unfortunately, as the year went on, it just got rougher. In June we became entangled in a significant community relations nightmare. One of Jenny's initial ideas was to host a weekly Dance Night on Saturdays from 11:00pm-1:30am. As it happened, this offering ended up being popular with the gay and lesbian community. Although it was well attended, there was not a corresponding uptick in sales. In addition, we were having a hard time staffing the later-than-usual shift, had received a negative customer comment about the vibe, and complaints from the neighborhood behind us that the music was too loud. We became weary of dealing with what felt like an on-going headache and decided to discontinue it. We immediately suffered an unexpected backlash of retaliation. We became the object of a vigorous postcard campaign and received countless cards all uniformly formatted.

Somethyme Management:

You say you don't want to see lesbians and gay men dancing in your restaurant. You must not want to see them eating, drinking, and spending money in your restaurant. So I'm eating someplace else and spending money I would normally have spent at Somethyme.

Today I chose not to eat at the Somethyme Restaurant to protest your homophobic policy. Instead, I ate at Rhumba's with 2 other persons. We spent approximately $20 there.

Right from the start of the restaurant many of our staff were gays and lesbians. Before this time, I had not actually known any gays or lesbians, or maybe I just didn't know that they were gay! But this all changed for me at Somethyme. Friendships were made as we worked alongside one another, hung out or played music together, and celebrated each other's birthdays. All the normal things you do with friends. Somethyme is where I began to understand that Love is Love, not in a lofty principled esoteric kind of way, but in a flesh and blood kind of way. Somethyme became known as a safe place to work, an accepting place to work, an affirming place to work. It was unnerving to be viewed now as an unwelcoming place.

It was public enough that Steve Schewel came to us, as publisher of *The Independent Weekly*, to let us know that the paper was considering doing an article about the issue, hoping that we could settle it before they pursued that action. Steve was a friend of both mine and Lise's; he was the first person I met at Duke, was married to a former employee, and was a friend of Elmer's. We were grateful he came to us, but felt like we were being accused unfairly.

Lise had the idea that we should formally meet with some of those upset and try to talk things through. This proved to be a great suggestion. The prevailing assumption was that the customer complaint was the sole reason we stopped. We were not uncomfortable with women dancing with women and men dancing with men. We were burdened by the problems of its staging and didn't want to be dealing with it anymore. It was a business decision, not a withholding of a blessing. We came to that shared understanding. We survived. *The Independent* didn't do their "exposé." But after the lukewarm acceptance of the renovation by our customer base in general, to be viewed as discriminatory by a group that had previously been highly supportive and whom we supported was depressing.

Somethyme vs. Anotherthyme

The second half of 1985 was one of intensifying rivalry between Somethyme and Anotherthyme, fueled by our own increasingly strained personal relationships. These days, I think that the outcome was inevitable.

Somethyme had been built on the menu and recipes Mary created. It was her food that people came for, her specials that kept them interested and engaged. After Mary sold her shares to Jenny, the new recipes and specials she once brought to Somethyme began to decrease, as did her presence. There were a couple of reasons why this could have been. One, Jenny, as a new owner, wanted to put her own stamp on the menu. And two, Mary may not have felt as obliged to contribute now that she was down to 10% ownership.

As her attention waned, we began to take note. We began to think that Mary had turned her back on us, washed her hands of us. We also began to consider that there was the possibility of, if not willful neglect, then actual sabotage.

And why not sabotage? Was not Somethyme's majority shareholder Mary's ex-husband's betrothed? It's not hard to imagine that there could have been psychological conflicts that Mary felt toward Jenny – that Mary may not have wanted Jenny to succeed and so withheld critical support.

And what about me? I began to see things through a persistent dark shadow. As Mary contributed less, my resentment grew. After years of keeping my emotions in check as far as Mary was concerned, I was finding it difficult to do so any longer. When troubled waters began to brew, I no longer wanted to be the one that tried to calm them down. I reached for the spoon; I turned up the heat. I know I had many conversations about Mary with Lise and Jenny and others which had, at its core, a deep seated and smoldering anger.

We can also add a change of life picture for me. Marielle, born mid-August, meant that the whole of 1985 was a time of pregnancy and post-partum motherhood. The personal stakes rose considerably. The need for the restaurant to support me and Tom and our child took on greater urgency.

Personality conflicts aside, dwindling sales may have been the mark of not enough business for two Thymes in Durham. Or maybe people simply preferred Mary's Anotherthyme, the food and the ambiance. To be considered second or to fear that we might be considered second in the affections of the public was debilitating.

Again I make the point: the life of Somethyme, its relationships both personal and business, were multi-layered and complicated. Financial insecurity heightens any disagreements. We were in a pressure cooker. We needed each other even as we sought independence. We were friends, we were partners, we were competitors. In any case, for whatever reason, a battle for the very existence of Somethyme, let alone its soul, was one we waged every day. The tension, real or imagined, there on its own or there because we created it, continued to mount. We were battle scarred and battle wearied, blinded by an insular and perhaps paranoid world view. It was not unlike a morality play to us: good vs evil. I don't know if that was the case at Anotherthyme. I don't know if Mary was deeply hurt when a valued employee of hers would leave Anotherthyme to come work with us or if she had a sense of exhilaration when someone left Somethyme to join her. I *can* say that the reverse was true.

It became difficult for us to concentrate on anything else. The only solution we were able to think of was to be free of Mary. Buying Mary out became a topic of conversation. Sometime during the summer, we approached her. I wrote in my journal on September 6 (three weeks after the birth of Marielle and while I was on maternity leave):

Jenny called to say that Mary had reversed herself again and decided that she would sell her remaining 10%, that she wanted her menu back December 1st and that she wanted the liability of the $50,000 loan off her house.

Lise is interested in buying the 10%.

According to Jenny, Mary feels very badly – is angry – feels pushed out, etc. Under ordinary circumstances I would be inclined to try to smooth the rough edges and make a better transition. But I too have resentful feelings toward Mary which I doubt would get resolved by talking with her.

This flipped back and forth over the course of the fall and kept us in a state of constant uncertainty. I think on these things now, from this distant perspective, without the passion of those long-gone moments, those layers of who knows what: jealousy, built-up hurt, feelings of loss of control, the need for success and the prospect of failure. And I think: Enough. Could the explanation simply be: it is not easy for people to get along for extended periods; it is hard to live with one another in Peace.

At this point, I pick up my photo albums to look at the pictures of us taken at the time. I see ones taken by my mother at the baby shower Jenny hosted for me, probably in June or July 1985, well into the time I have just described. I see Mary there – part of the celebration. All of us there together: Jill, Jenny, Lise, Mary. All of us looking young and beautiful with no sorrow in our eyes or hint of resentments brewing.

Where is the truth in all of this? Can all of it be true at the same time? Is it the at-easeness with each other which seems captured in the photographs? Or was that us on good behavior? I don't think it was just us playing nice. I think it was real. A couple of pages later in the album, I come to a picture of Mary and Helen Griffin at our house coming to see Marielle for the first time, when she was just a week old. Mary was there because she cared.

Jenny and Jill; photo by Ann Rocap, 1985

Lise, Suzanne Sturm (behind Lise), me, Helen Griffin; photo by Ann Rocap, 1985

Me, Marielle, Mary, and Helen; photo by Tom Prince, 1985

Sometime in late fall, I was tasked to have a conversation with Mary that Jenny, Lise, and I hoped would settle things. And maybe it did. I remember proposing that Mary consider a paradigm shift. Could she, would she, view the sale not as one in which she was being forced out of the restaurant against her wishes but rather of her letting the restaurant go of her own accord? Lise was prepared to buy the shares if Mary would relinquish them. My line of thought was that Mary had been freeing herself of Somethyme ever since she opened Anotherthyme, even more so when she sold her shares to Jenny. We were asking her to give over the final bit.

Eventually we came to an agreement, much as I laid out in my journal but with these critical additions: she did not want us to use the name Somethyme for the restaurant after the sale and she did not want us to use the Somethyme recipes. As part of the settlement we had to turn over the recipe box to her. (Although I did retain copies, as did many staff members, I did not have a complete set.)

The transition occurred over the New Year; the papers officially signed on January 24, 1986. Lise bought Mary's 10% and the three of us essentially opened a whole new restaurant. Somehow we thought we were up to the challenge; we knew it was a risk but it was a risk we were willing to take. It was far riskier than we imagined.

What Was Going On in 1986?

NATIONAL & INTERNATIONAL NEWS EVENTS:
- Ronald Reagan was President;
- Mad Cow Disease broke out in Britain;
- The Iran-Contra Affair was exposed;
- The US bombed Libya;
- The Space Shuttle Challenger disintegrated after launch, killing all onboard (we watched this from the new bar's TV);
- IBM unveiled the first laptop computer;
- Internet Mail Access Protocol was defined for e-mail;
- The Human Genome Project was launched; and
- The Chernobyl Nuclear Power Station disaster.

WE WATCHED THESE MOVIES:
- Top Gun
- Crocodile Dundee
- Platoon
- The Karate Kid, Part II
- Star Trek IV: The Voyage Home
- Aliens

WE LISTENED TO THESE MUSICIANS:
- Billy Joel
- Robert Palmer
- Lionel Richie
- Van Halen
- The Police
- Debbie Harry
- Whitney Houston
- The Pretenders
- Genesis

- Prince (oh yes, *Purple Rain*)
- Culture Club
- Bruce Springsteen

WE WATCHED THESE TV SHOWS:
- Magnum, P.I.
- Miami Vice
- Hill Street Blues
- Cheers (in which local Josh Lozoff had a recurring role)
- Family Ties
- Murder, She Wrote (in which our own Lawrence Bullock had a small part)
- The Cosby Show

THE COST OF THINGS:
- Yearly Inflation Rate: 1.91%
- Median Price of an Existing Home: $80,300;
- Average Annual Income: $22,400;
- Average Monthly Rent: $385;
- 1 gallon of gas: 89 cents;
- A computer: $1,599;
- A dozen eggs: 87 cents;
- Ford Mustang $7,452;
- Minimum Wage: $3.35; and
- The Unemployment Rate: 7%.

THESE WORDS WERE ADDED TO THE DICTIONARY:
- Bungee jump: an activity that involves a person jumping from a great height while connected to a large elastic cord;
- Crackhead: a person who habitually takes crack cocaine;
- Cringy: causing feelings of embarrassment or awkwardness;
- Goths: A culture and manner of dress developed by fans of gothic rock, an offshoot of the post – punk music genre. The

style most often includes dark (usually solid black) attire, dark makeup, and black hair;

- HIV;
- Junk email;
- Ozone layer: a region of Earth's stratosphere that absorbs most of the sun's ultraviolet radiation;
- PC (Politically Correct);
- Portobello: a type of mushroom;
- Sippy cup: a drinking cup designed for toddlers which prevents or reduces spills; and
- Sport Utility Vehicle (SUV): A passenger car built on a truck chassis.

Seventh Street

If we couldn't be Somethyme anymore, what would we be? We needed a new name. Jill's husband, Bill, came up with a brilliant one: Seventh Street. Broad Street had, in fact, been called 7th Street on the old city plat maps. 9th Street was two blocks over. The most inspired ad for the new place was: *Somethymes change is good for you.*

If I apply the same question/answer/rubric to the name of Seventh Street as I did to Somethyme, Seventh Street is also a revealing answer. As the answer to the question "Where?" Seventh Street is definitive, clear, and not mysterious. The goals for Seventh Street were a far cry from the ambitious and visionary ideals we had for Somethyme. In January 1986, the fact that we were opening a restaurant that was *ours* was reason enough. Its singular characteristic was that it was *not-Mary's*. The *not-Mary's* meant that we were more about what we weren't than about what we were. I say that now. Back then we did not consider such things; an underlying mission statement did not seem important, so focused were we on coming up with the required new menu.

The public had some confusion over the name change and ownership – seemingly coming overnight. One day Somethyme, the next day Seventh Street. There was no change in staff, no change in décor; the outer trimmings remained the same. Fred Benton, a restaurant critic, wrote of this aspect in his June review of the restaurant for *The Durham Morning Herald*, six months after our opening:

> *When these four young women decided to purchase Somethyme from previous owner Mary Bacon and make it their own with a new name, they caught the public by surprise. Even now patrons aren't certain whether or not the old Somethyme still exists.*

His explanation of the transition was annoyingly wrong, but there you go. Our goal, was primarily that of maintaining the culinary niche we had carved out at Somethyme. There is no mention of supporting the arts, promoting progressive causes, being a catalyst for change; there are no lofty principles. According to the article, we wanted to:

- maintain our emphasis on vegetarian foods but also include chicken and seafood, especially in the specials;
- keep using the freshest and highest quality ingredients;
- maintain a friendly atmosphere for our customers;
- promote International Weekends looking to other cultures for culinary ideas; and to
- keep the middle-price area of the menu interesting. He quotes Jill as saying: ". . . *the culinary imagination has no price tag, and the palate should be as enlivened by a $7 entrée as a $14 one.*"

I don't have documentation of how we told the staff of Somethyme's demise and Seventh Street's birth. We did have a "Christening Party" for Seventh Street on January 4, 1986, and on the following day rolled out our new menu and began anew. I do not have a single menu, aside from the weekend specials, from this era. The cook's notes scarcely take notice of the transition of ownership – only the major undertaking of the menu change.

For the dinner menu, we came up with ten entrees: Spinach Lasagna, Three Bean Burritos, Tostadas, Chicken Enchiladas, Ratatouille & Fried Grits, Chicken Parmesan, Chicken Marsala, Moo Shu Shrimp, Pasta with Scallops & Saffron Sauce, and a Seafood of the Day.

For salads we offered: Niçoise (tuna, egg, potatoes, green beans, Kalamata olives, tomatoes, lemon wedges on romaine lettuce), Tabbouleh, Chicken Salad, and the customary Design Your Own. Our salad dressings were: Roquefort, Russian Creole, Tofu Tahini (an obvious knock-off of Lemon Tamari), and a Dijon Mustard Vinaigrette.

At lunch we started with 14 items, eight of them sandwiches including:

Mediterranean Tuna, Chicken Salad, Egg Salad, Pimiento Cheese, and Rodger's Millet Burger, our effort at replacing the Beanburger. The Millet Burger had been served at the Sallam, a restaurant co-owned by Rodger Tygard, Billy Stevens, and Brother Yusuf, which had closed. Rodger, the drummer of Mobile City, offered it to us, and we gratefully accepted. It was very good and much easier to make than the Beanburger. We also served up Boboli (an individual pizza), Tostadas, a daily Omelette, and Shrimp Fried Rice.

Our Brunch Menu included: pecan sticky buns, croissants, bagels, ambrosia fruit salad, Omelettes: Herb, Country (cheddar, hash browns with green peppers), South of the Border (pepper jack cheese, onions and tomatoes, topped with guacamole and sour cream), Norwegian (cream cheese, lox, tomatoes, sautéed onion, dill); Griddle Foods: Buttermilk Cakes, Rice Pancakes, French Toast, Potato Pancakes with fried apples; Eggs Florentine; and Pecan Waffles.

In the Kitchen PC Notes on January 13, the first notes after opening up as Seventh Street, I began by saying:

The first order of business is a commendation to everyone for getting through the first week of the new menu. I was really impressed by the good spirits and hard work you all put out. For such a big change, things went very smoothly. Thank you.

I end the notes with:

Again, you have done a wonderful job coping with the new menu, disordered kitchen, and tired bosses, MR

In between are three pages of instructions, notes on garnishes, how many pieces pita bread should be cut into, and on and on. I apologize by saying, "*These notes are not going to be very organized. There is so much to cover, please bear with me.*"

Actually, I think we did a pretty good job coming up with ideas for a new menu. We also introduced an assortment of new breads which I developed: Tomato-Basil, Dill, and Cinnamon-Raisin, in addition to the Mixed Grain. I was proud of the Pomodoro Basilico sandwich which was my own invention (marinated mozzarella, tomato, avocado, grilled mushrooms, pesto mayonnaise, and lettuce on Tomato-Basil Bread). However, it was hard to keep up with the baking and hard to keep up with the many items on the menu.

Later that month, when the papers were officially signed, Jenny and David, Lise and Charlie, Jill and Bill, and Tom and I celebrated by going out to dinner at The Orient Express in Chapel Hill. Within the first six months of 1986, Jenny offered a portion of her shares to Lise and Jill, so, by June, we had become the four owners mentioned by Fred Benton.

We enjoyed the monthly international weekends, from Thai-themed with Jenny's inspired Thai Rice Noodles (stuffed Boston lettuce leaves with a peanut dipping sauce) – a totally fun dish to make and eat – to Italian during which we played a tape of Puccini's *Madame Butterfly* to create a special ambiance. We got good press. This review is from *The Independent*, edition October 24-November 6, 1986:

The food is both inexpensive and uniformly excellent, with an emphasis on exotic dishes . . . The wine list is large, well chosen, and reasonable priced . . . The tuna (a special) that I ordered was grilled and seasoned perfectly, and the sautéed potatoes were slightly crisp on the outside and attractively presented. My companion's pasta with scallops was flawless: the pasta al dente, the scallops tender, and the saffron subtle and interesting. For dessert we shared a generous serving of splendid blueberry strudel, and the decaffeinated coffee, freshly brewed, was excellent.

Our intentions were good, but those good intentions were not enough to carry us through. The truth is that restaurant work is a grind – a constant time and energy suck. After the hard fought year of 1985, 1986 was a harsh dose of reality leading both Jenny and Lise to withdraw in 1987. My cook's meeting notes from January 16, 1987, simply remarked:

> *Jill and I are trying to get out of our scheduled shifts as we pick up the pieces that Jenny and Lise were holding.*

It is unclear to me now whether that was a temporary absence or a permanent one. But my language has the sound of weary permanence to it. Both Lise and Jenny did leave some time in the first half of the year. Lise took another job (Regulator Press); she retained her shares.

Jenny came to the conclusion that her foray into the restaurant business was not to her liking. She had other business ideas she wanted to pursue (a shoe retail shop among them), and if she felt like being involved in a restaurant she could always help David at Pyewacket. At the end of May, Jenny wrote that she was offering to sell her shares to the corporation. If the corporation did not want them, she would offer them to Jill or me. She did not have a preference. She wrote on May 30, 1987:

Well girls, I have, for the most part, good memories, shining moments, close times, distant times, lovely times, hilarious times – it's all a patchwork in a chapter called taking risks.

Through it all I'll always be glad I had the experience of working with all of you – fighting the fights – making changes – scrubbing mussels with pregnant ladies, making the world's worst Paella and keeping up with the Thymes. Next time around I'll find a good fit.

Love you all, Jenny

In that letter she also details her financial status with Seventh Street: payment due for the shares sold to Jill and Lise, payment due on a loan she had extended to the restaurant, and the potential sale of the remainder of her shares. (Both Jill and I did buy those shares, splitting them down the middle. I had to borrow money from my folks to make the purchase.) While this was an amicable departure, the upshot was that it was now just up to Jill and me. To be sure, Jill was full of ideas and had a lot of energy and drive. You could argue that we were in need of big ideas because the old ideas we had were no longer working, hadn't been working for a long time. We had the debt of the expansion, dropping sales, and I didn't have anything left, other than keep on giving it everything I had: time and hard work, trying to keep things going, each day, every day.

Looking back on the cook notes and the specials menus, it is shocking (to me now) how far our menu became slanted to meats during this time. We went from adding chicken in 1984 to serving hot dogs, hamburgers, Reuben sandwiches, ribeye steaks, pork chops, and lamb kebobs by 1987 either as regular offerings or as specials. Maybe it was a sign of the times or maybe that was how our tastes were running, but it was a marked departure from our vegetarian roots.

We began having international weekends every weekend rather than once a month. To supplement recipes Jenny and the staff developed in 1986, I would commonly spend (my day off) Tuesday in the library downtown researching and coming up with menus and recipes which we would implement on Friday.

Eventually we had recipes for rotating weekends of Thai, German, Soviet, Cuban, Indian, Cajun, Viennese, Australian, French, Moroccan, Swiss, Irish, Caribbean, Italian, Chinese, Hawaiian, Ethiopian, Austrian, Mexican. We had American Regional Weekends: Cape Cod, Charleston, Southern, Tex-Mex; and Seasonal Weekends: Early Spring, Summer Solstice, Winter, Thanksgiving, Valentine's Day.

The early years of Somethyme had a fixed menu, and the tasks necessary for keeping that going were knowable and regular. There was a sauce schedule; Beanburger was always made on Wednesdays. As the recipes and procedures became ingrained, we began to offer more specials. Seventh Street, by contrast, suffered by having so many international weekends with constantly changing specials. In addition, we were experimenting with the menu a lot, trying to define and develop our niche or frankly, find it. All this made it hard to feel accomplished and was exhausting.

WEEKEND SPECIALS AT 7th STREET

AUGUST		SEPTEMBER	
	7/31 & 8/1 BANGLEDESH		4 & 5 INDIAN
	7 & 8 HOT SUMMER DAYS		11 & 12 GREEK
	14 & 15 MOROCCAN		
	21 & 22 SPANISH		18 & 19 MEXICAN
	28 & 29 CARRIBEAN		25 & 26 INDIAN SUMM.
OCTOBER		NOVEMBER	
	2 & 3 INDIAN		6 & 7 SOVIET
	9 & 10 ITALIAN		
	16 & 17 CAJUN		13 & 14 FRENCH
	23 & 24 THAI		20 & 21 CAPE COD
	30 & 31 CUISINE FROM SLEEPY HOLLOW		27 & 28 THANKSGIVING

The restaurant scene in Durham was also becoming more competitive; more and more trendy restaurants were opening up. In addition to Anotherthyme, there were Sudi's and 5 Points downtown, Magnolia Grill right around the corner in the old Wellspring Grocery location, Papagayo's on Erwin Road, Mr. Harvey's Bistro on the Boulevard, as well as others. When Somethyme opened, the word chef – as opposed to cook – was not in parlance. Over the years, the role of chef and the perceived importance of having a chef or being a chef, began to carry greater weight in the restaurant's ability to succeed. Mary achieved that designation at Anotherthyme. Somethyme was always a place that had good cooks (with Mary as high priestess). I think during the Somethyme era, that was enough. But during the Seventh Street years, not having a chef was a deficit. We all contributed me, Jenny, Jill, the kitchen managers and cooks – but it wasn't enough.

Jill began to advertise heavily. The ads were quite clever: "All Roads Lead to the Street" (drawing attention to our international fare), "Get Out of the Street" and "Quick" (early lunch-to-go pitches), "Come To Seventh Heaven" (for Valentine's Day), and "Go Play in the Street" (promoting the bar and watching sports on the TV). These ads did bring in more customers, but the additional people only paid for the advertising itself and did not translate into extra money going toward the bottom line. We began having price specials hoping to entice a stronger or more regular clientele. Again, this resulted in more people, but they were paying us less money.

And then, there was the aptly named "Under the Street" undertaking. 1102 & 1104 Broad Street had two floors: a top floor which we were using and a basement that we were not, but was available to us. Since music had always been one of our strong suits, Jill proposed turning this area into a music club, building a stage and bar and installing a stairway down into it from the outside. Her strategy for paying for it, without taking out another bank loan which we could ill afford, was to pitch the concept to individual friends and supporters each of whom would loan us $1,000. We were to pay them back in a year's time, and they would be given free tickets for shows in the meanwhile.

There was a lot of excitement about Under the Street. This quote is from a *Durham Morning Herald* article dated April 24, 1987: "*Under the Street will be the sort of establishment Durham has lacked – one principally oriented to live entertainment, presenting a regular schedule of touring acts and select local talent.*" The internet site *Open Durham* describes it as being an "*indie/punk/jazz venue*" and includes a comment that it was "*quite important to the underground/alternative music scene of Durham.*"

We raised at least $17,000 this way and created Under the Street. Jill did go on to book national acts including Sun Ra, Koko Taylor,

Reverend Billy C. Wirtz, and Johnny Winter, in addition to local bands.

Somethyme's Change
Wasn't Good for Me, After All

At some point, the restaurant began to host New Year's Eve
Celebrations with a post-midnight breakfast buffet and a band
playing til the wee hours. Mobile City Band was the band scheduled to
play on December 31, 1987, which included me. That week, Jill casually
informed me that she had agreed to provide hors d'oeuvres for 100
people at Carolina Theatre's New Year's Eve event. The owner,
Stephen Barefoot, an Under the Street donor, had made some kind of
trade for them. I was used to solving a problem by throwing time at it.
But this catering job required more than time. It was a lot of product
to come up with on short notice. At the time we were cash strapped,
and I didn't feel I could just go out and buy special ingredients to
support the swap. Nor did I want to add hours to the payroll by asking
staff to help me. So I came in early and began making as much as I
could with what I could find: stuffed cherry tomatoes, stuffed figs,
cucumber and smoked salmon sandwiches, and such. All day long I
worked, and as I worked, I knew it was going to be insufficient. Sure
enough, shortly after I made the delivery, Stephen called to complain
about the paltry amount of food provided. It was one of the most
humiliating conversation of my life. Jill remedied the situation by
agreeing to refund his $1,000 loan to Under the Street. Jill did this
without casting any sign of judgment or blame towards me.

Nevertheless, I was deeply ashamed and completely demoralized. I
was already at the end of my rope. Four days earlier, in my journal on
Sunday, December 27, I had written *"I want to make a rough draft of my
resignation."* Now here I was sitting in the middle of the basement
stairs in a stupor, in a haze, in despair. I was exhausted by the day's
work, burdened by the failure of that activity, and daunted by the
prospect of a performance with Mobile City coming up in just a few

hours. I had thrown all the time I had, and more, at that job, at Somethyme, at Seventh Street. I was spent and empty. That afternoon, the last day of the year, I came to a place where I keenly felt a sense of betrayal. Both of being betrayed and of betraying.

The days of being able to get by on $25 a week were long gone. Tom and I had a child, we had a mortgage. The fact that the restaurant was becoming more and more risky was becoming harder and harder to ignore. But above all, I was depleted. The following day I began writing that letter detailing my intent to sell my shares. On February 28, 1988, Jill agreed to buy them.

Her letter stating this included these generous words:

I love you, Mary, and I hope that the next several months will provide us both with the insights and resources we need to fulfill both our work and personal goals.   Jill

Relieved of management ownership (but not paid for my shares), I continued to do the bookwork and baking on the weekend. Laura Hickok helped me find a part-time job at Duke Hospital which I kept until the birth of our second child, Christiana, in June of 1989. I also got a part-time bookkeeping job at Blacknall Memorial Presbyterian Church.

The restaurant continued on a downward spiral, and in August of 1990 Seventh Street filed for bankruptcy. As a creditor with an outstanding loan to the restaurant, I was appointed by the court to the Creditors' Committee along with Jay Miller and John Havran, both of whom were friends of mine and of the restaurant, and were also owed money. The function of a Creditors' Committee is to represent the overall interests of all unsecured creditors. (Jenny was still owed money but she was a secured creditor meaning her loan was backed by the property or assets in the restaurant.) I didn't want to sign the agreement to take less than what was owed, even though that was what was expected. I still thought it was possible that Jill with her tenacity and drive could be successful in turning things around and if so, why not get paid in full. But Jay and John did not think that was likely and, it just isn't the way these bankruptcy agreements go. It was awkward to be on the committee with such a long history of being an owner and therefore bearing no small degree of responsibility for the state of affairs.

In November of 1991, my relationship with Somethyme / Seventh Street came to an abrupt end. When I went in to collect the bookwork and payroll time sheets I found instead a small note taped to each pile from Jill to me. A terse statement informed me that each of those tasks was now assigned elsewhere: Aden would take over the bookwork (some kind of symmetry there); Lise, the payroll. Beyond the fact that it was not a face-to-face communication was that each of the notes was written on a small slip of scrap paper, almost like she couldn't be troubled to find a fresh piece of paper and so just pulled something out of the trash can. Nor was it a private communication, the notes would have been visible to anyone who came into the office. It was a particularly stunning and casual pink slip.

11·18·91

MR -

Aden has taken over journal sheet activity as of 1st of November. He will take care of state forms & filings in future. I gave him your estimate work from 1st week in Oct. He'll adjust for it in November.

JC

11·18·91

MR.

Lise has volunteered to do the payroll for us. Given our need to save every dollar we can I need to take her up on her offer. Please do the payroll for the 22nd & 29th. Lise will take over after that.

JC

I walked out of the office, through the restaurant, and when the 1104 Broad Street door closed behind me, I shook the dirt from my shoes. Although Jill asked me to do the two upcoming payrolls, I called Lise and said that I didn't have it within me to comply with that request. I never went back. I heard the news that Seventh Street had closed in June of 1993 for failure to pay taxes from a third-hand source.

The End of the Story

What am I, what are we, to take away from this story, this history?

To be sure, there is a certain chronology of descent. Through troubled times and unstable finances, our attention strayed. Drawn into skirmishes of one kind or another, we were distracted from tending to the health and welfare of the restaurant itself. The multiple dramas of workers vs. owners, union-leaning staff vs. shareholders, Somethyme vs. Anotherthyme, and the transition of Somethyme into Seventh Street all took their own psychic toll. These dramas consumed our attention handicapping our ability to conduct the business of running the business.

As the collective memory of Somethyme grew distant, we lost the common thread with our past. The flavor or feel that had begun to change toward the end of Somethyme picked up its pace and intensity during Seventh Street. The encroachment of meat into the menu is one example. Music is another. We went from a gentle acoustic folk vibe to a harder, grungier electric rock-and-roll and punk scene. Under the Street brought an edginess we never had had before. We never had to hire bouncers at Somethyme.

Going from Restaurant to Restaurant & Bar at the time of the expansion brought a certain darkness which became more noticeable in the Seventh Street years as the finances became more unstable. Bar revenue became a bigger and more important piece of the financial pie.

And, I think we lost our feminine identity. Through the years, as the business evolved, those who became partners or owners were all women and most of our managers, front and back, were as well: Dorothy Jackson, Teresa Jones, Linda King, Pat Marterer, Suzanne Sturm. We were strongly feminine. Since my right hand man was

Tom, maybe you could say the loss of the feminine identity began with me, but it became more pronounced during Jill's tenure. Her right and left hands, as well as, right and left feet (kitchen, front, bar, Under the Street) were men. We were no longer a mostly-female enterprise.

Slowly the dream of community was replaced with a desperate need for customers. We lost the connection to our stakeholders: staff and community supporters. We fell out of relationship with ourselves. We no longer espoused our once firmly held ethical, ecological, social, spiritual, and political values. The passions of our early days were replaced with job descriptions and transactions at the cash register. When hard times came, we no longer had the depth of support nor the personal resilience to meet them head on.

When Jill and I became business partners, she gave me a small polished rose quartz stone. She said she was giving it to me as a promise. Stones have acquired meanings over time. A rose quartz has come to represent universal and unconditional love and the color pink, gentleness, calmness, femininity, and compassion. She meant to be a good partner. And I think she tried to be one. I believe she saw her job to be that of keeping Seventh Street open however she could, and she tried everything she could think of, used all the tools in her tool box. She did, actually, extend the life of the restaurant. But Seventh Street was an uphill struggle burdened by years of accumulated weight, Somethyme's as well as its own, which, in the end, were simply too heavy be lifted, let alone carried. I still have that quartz and I when I look at it I don't think of it as a promise broken – I think of it as a promise made in good faith.

As it happened, it was all Jill at the end; she was the last one standing and she took the fall, unflinchingly, by herself.

When things go wrong, it's natural to ask yourself "What if . . . ?" and

I, ask myself too:

- What if I been emotionally stronger and hadn't sold my shares in 1976?
- What if we hadn't expanded?
- What if Mary hadn't sold her shares to Jenny?
- What if we hadn't added chicken and Coca-Cola, burgers and salami; and
- What if we hadn't opened Under the Street?

All these "What Ifs" represent a bit of idle and wasted thinking. The fact is, it is what happened. Maybe we were just a 1970s-vibe restaurant that was unable to transition into the 1980s and 1990s. Maybe we could have transitioned, but we lost our way. Getting lost, getting off track happens to the best of us, and we were the best of us. Every day had so much work in it that it became hard to look outside ourselves or within ourselves for the *why* we were doing the *what* we were doing. Every day had more in it than could be accomplished. And yet, there remains some balance and beauty in all of this. We had a string of good years and a string of not so good years, all of them filled with hard work, all of them essentially the feeding ministry that Elmer referred to in *The Chronicle* article before we started. There is inherent value in preparing food to be served for the nourishment of others. We always prepared the food with care and pride.

I don't want to give the impression that I consider Somethyme and Seventh Street failures, because I don't. Yes, there was a beginning and yes, there was an end: a birth and a death. But there was also life, and that life lives on in memory and it lives on in relationships. Almost twenty years was a huge accomplishment. In truth, we defied the odds. We didn't know, going into it, that the average life span of a restaurant is five years and that as many as 80% fail in the first year. It was a glorious experiment. We are held in high esteem by so many people: staff and customers, musicians and artists. The fact is that Somethyme (and I fold in Seventh Street here) is still a life-giving force, even now. Friendships were made that are still sound. Skills were learned that have been used in other settings and passed on. Budding artists and musicians were encouraged and have gone on to create great work. We can look back and say that what we did had a holiness to it because we acknowledged and attached deep meaning and purpose to the work we undertook.

I have also tried to understand my own evolution. Eighteen years was a big chunk of my life. For me, Somethyme was a rite of passage; Seventh Street the kind of badge you get when you are wounded in battle but survive. Because this is a telling of my story, this story includes my struggles with leadership. I didn't love power. I loved the work; I loved the place; I loved the people I worked with.

If I try to parse out what was personally redemptive about the Seventh Street years, I come up with this list. It was:

- an experience that Tom and I shared;
- a place that sheltered and supported our little family, albeit not dependably; and it was
- a time during which I grew in my knowledge and expertise as a cook and manager.

I did, after a bit, land on my feet. In August 1992, a year after Whole Foods had acquired Wellspring, former Somethymer, Portia McKnight, recruited me to be the Prepared Foods Team Leader at the Whole Foods Chapel Hill Store where she was Store Team Leader and where Somethymer Dave Steere (who had run for PC) was her Associate. This job offer came at a very needful time, when Tom and I were barely making ends meet.

Our heater had given out in early March. This meant we had neither heat nor hot water. We could not afford to replace the unit for eight months, or until November just before Thanksgiving. We were moving an electric heater from room to room as needed, heating water on the stove for baths. We were miserable. So it didn't take much convincing that this would be a stabilizing job for us. And it was. It was hard work, but I received two Whole Foods National All-Star Team Leader Awards and one Honorable Mention in my four years in that job. In the recommendation for the 1995 All Star Award, Don Moffitt, then the President of the Whole Foods Southeast Region, wrote this about me:

In all of the company there is no Team Leader with as much responsibility as Mary Rocap. That's a bold statement, but consider – she has responsibility for over eighty team members . . . her area does about 22% of store sales, virtually all of the food . . . made in her kitchen . . . We [had] projected that the Kitchen would lose ground because of their strong performance in 1994. They didn't – Kitchen sales increased 6.24%. She made all four [quarterly] margin [targets], increased her Gross Profit Dollars 17% and placed first in regional All-Star criteria in five out of six categories.

I transferred over to the regional warehouse as an accountant in 1996 and would have held that position forever, but in 2002 Whole Foods closed it down.

During this time at the warehouse, my own music began to claim my attention. In the mid-1990s instead of singing songs others had written, I found I had songs within me longing to be sung. I began to write them. I received an Artist's Fellowship from the North Carolina Arts Council (grant year 2000/2001) for my songwriting. That fellowship came with substantial funding. From this, I recorded my first CD, "Sweet Mimosa." Since then I have recorded three other CDs of original material, my romp around the seasons: "Indian Summer," "Deep December Dreams," and finally "Spring: The Wind's Story," recorded in 2017. I also have a CD of hymns, "Hallelujah! Amen." Lise and Charlie are featured in these recordings, as well as my two daughters, my sister, and her daughters who sing with me.

In 2006, I began working at St. Matthew's Episcopal Church, in Hillsborough. This job pulled together everything I'd ever learned or been interested in. It fulfilled a vocational call to be actively involved in a community of faith. In the role of Parish Administrator, I used my bookkeeping skills and organizational skills daily. I was not intimidated when asked to provide a small lunch for the Bishop or a lunch for 100 following a Lenten Ecumenical Service. (And let me boast that I prepared many meals for the Presiding Bishop of the Episcopal Church, the Right Rev. Michael Curry, when he came to St. Matthew's for his Quiet Days during his years as the Bishop of North Carolina.) I was able to offer music for special services. I co-founded and continue to lead the St. Matthew's Women's Singing Circle, which has met monthly since 2009 for sacred singing within a service of Evening Prayer. And I founded St. Matthew's Faith & Arts Series which, in my tenure as Coordinator, brought over 100 events of song, poetry, drama, literature, film, and visual art exhibits to the parish and wider community. All of these pieces: the food, the art, the community, the logistics were part of the initial drive to open Somethyme. There is a clear line in my life from the one to the other. All essentially positive. All actually a blessing.

Some time ago, I began feeling a softening come into my heart for Mary, whom I had not seen in some years. One afternoon, I was at Costco and heard this voice calling out, "Is that my sweet Mary?" It was Mary. She called me sweet, her sweet Mary. Not her bitter, vindictive former partner Mary. She didn't turn away and go down another aisle, which I might have been inclined to do. She reached out, radiating friendship, forgiveness and acceptance. How like her, believing in the sweetness of our relationship and remembering it that way.

And here's something else that brightened me up considerably: Stephen Barefoot, the symbol of my New Year's Eve breaking point, was a guest at The Murphey School Radio Show, a yearly production featuring the "Wit, Lit, and Music" of North Carolina that raises funds for non-profits in Durham and Orange County. I've been an enthusiastic participant in the show, the creation of Georgann Eubanks and Donna Campbell, singing songs of my own from time to time and also jingles for show sponsors. Stephen, no longer involved with Carolina Theatre, was there as the manager of actor and playwright Mike Wiley, a featured guest. In the Green Room before the performance, he mentioned that my name was familiar to him. With trepidation, I reminded him of my role in the disaster of his 1987 New Year's Eve Celebration. I confessed the whole awful back story of my poor performance. He stated that he did not recall that episode and saw no need for me to recall it either. With a wave of his hand he released me from my burden and shame.

Sweet Forgiveness

Those two episodes have come to signify something deeply meaningful to me: they represent forgiveness. I received a blessing of forgiveness from Mary and from Stephen, which suggested it was time to forgive myself and time to forgive others. As I have written, although Somethyme and Seventh Street may have failed financially, I do not consider them failures, cautionary tales perhaps, but not at the core failures. However, I have carried around a certain amount of regret, a lingering sense of guilt, for having failed them, for having failed my partners. Not a failure of time and effort, but a failure to keep the faith through it all, to keep faithful to the commitments I made to them and to the restaurant.

A partner makes promises. I made promises. True, these were civil in nature, but all promises have a spiritual dimension. A promise is a pledge, a word of honor. The ideals and aspirations of the founding of the restaurant were not unlike the Baptismal Covenant found in the Book of Common Prayer of the Episcopal Church. In particular, I find a commonality in this question the Bishop asks a person about to be baptized: *Will you strive for justice and peace among all people, and respect the dignity of every human being?* To which one answers: *I will, with God's help.*

Weren't we all about Peace and Justice? Weren't we all about saving the world, treating everyone with respect? Along with Elmer and Mary, I pledged myself to these things through the practice of opening and running a restaurant. It was a promise made public when we printed our welcome statement on the menu. Sadly, we got mired in the muck of making the promise real. I was part of that failure – the failure to keep Somethyme strong enough that it could be those good things and could bring those good things to our community, to the world.

It's often said, you should forgive and forget. Perhaps forgive and release is a better way to say it. In worship, there is a ritual order. It starts with making a Confession. What follows are Gifts: the Absolution of Guilt, the Bestowal of Forgiveness, and the Blessing of Peace after which one is sent out into the world to try again, with a clean slate. This ritual order is applicable to any situation where there has been a break in fellowship or a wrong committed, be it with God, with another, with one's community, or with oneself.

If I seek forgiveness, for myself, for the restaurant as a whole, I need to acknowledge and confess that there were things I did and things I said that were damaging and that there were things I could have done and things I could have said that might have made a difference. The same can be said for the restaurant, both as an entity and as a group of individuals. This writing details some of them. We were, we are, all of us, flawed. I didn't, we didn't, get it right and the seeds of our wrongs were its undoing.

With Forgiveness comes Peace. But Peace is not the endgame; it is given (and received) with a Charge or Mandate to take that peace into the world and do the work God gives us to do. This work was perhaps expressed best by the prophet Micah: *"God has told you, O mortal, what is good, and what does the LORD require of you but to do justice, and to love kindness and to walk humbly with your God?"* (Micah 6:8)

I believe Somethyme and Seventh Street was the work given to me during the years of my life between 1973 and 1991. Somethyme had a vision to be an alternative to the commercial profit-seeking institutions the world has plenty of. It offered itself as a place for community which the world has precious little of. It was not altogether different from the vision of that 8th Century BCE prophet, Micah. The world we live in needs more Justice, more Kindness, more

Humbleness. It needs these qualities more now than ever. I want to keep working on those goals, and with God's help, I will.

Somethyme's vision is still one that I believe in. No, we didn't succeed in being a business that still exists today. No, we didn't succeed in achieving our goals of world peace, racial reconciliation, social justice, consensus amongst a staff of 20 persons about the beer list, or even just getting along with each other, but they were worthy aspirations.

We all have work given us. Work using our own particular gifts and talents, in our own particular place and time, within our own daily circles of contact. Those circles of being extend far into the world. All of our work can be endowed with a higher purpose if we so choose. Elmer, Mary, and I sat in a booth at The Ivy Room and founded Somethyme based on the desire to, yes, begin a restaurant, but also to align our work with principles that were bigger than we were. I don't want to forgive and forget. I want to forgive and be forgiven, release and be released, remember, reflect, and reengage in that work, even with my dimming eyesight and creaky joints. To that end, I raise my glass to each and every one of you and propose this toast: "Here's to a round of forgiveness. Drink up. The taste is sweet."

With that sweet cup in hand, I take my leave, bringing my recounting to an end. To my founding partners who are, in 2022, thankfully still here, Elmer Hall and Mary Bacon: We did something good. I'm so proud of what we created. You changed my life for the better. To Mary: the only continual owner of Somethyme, thank you for keeping the restaurant together during the years you had no partner. To Martha Maiden, Jenny Wears, Lise Uyanik Ebel, and Jill Cotter: Thank you for your partnership and giving yourself to the place as you did. And to everybody else who walked through the door of 1104 Broad Street hoping the place offered more than just a job: Thank you for whatever part you played – your contributions large and small – thanks for being there.

In closing, I've paraphrased one of our welcoming statements into one of farewell:

Shalom.

We were once a working community who loved to cook, serve and eat fine natural food. We prepared meals with care and creativity for the enjoyment and good health of others. We were a meeting place for the wider community where we all celebrated life and rejoiced in the goodness of the Earth.

Amen and Amen. May blessings upon blessings be upon you,

Mary

Addendums

- WHAT DREAMS?
- SOMETHYME'S 30TH REUNION
- WHO WORKED THERE?
- THE 2019 ANNIVERSARY POST ON FACEBOOK
- VENDORS AND PRODUCTS
- SOME PEOPLE
- SOME RECIPES
- ACKNOWLEDGEMENTS

What Dreams?

I regularly dream about Somethyme. The dreams generally fall into two categories: one, I am a stove cook preparing for dinner and nothing is ready; two, I come to the restaurant and realize that I don't know if I should be working or not. I know I have not been there in a long time but am not sure if I am still responsible for something that needs doing, or if others have assumed I am doing something that I am not.

The "Dinner Cook" one makes sense to me because all our entrees depended on rice or baked potatoes. They were either done or they were not done. A lot rode on that fact. Both took an hour's time to prepare. So if you were late and came in after 4:00, if someone else had not turned on the oven or started the rice for you, it was going to be a rough shift.

The "Am I Supposed to be at Work?" dream makes sense too. I think it shows the uncertainty I had about my relationship to the place. Even when I pulled out, I was always being pulled back in. Even when I was not responsible, I always felt responsible.

Here is one of those: I enter the kitchen (in the current time). It has been rented out and redesigned as an art gallery. The walls are now a beautiful deep aqua color, but I can still imagine it as it used to be: the stove here; the walk-in there. The steps to the mezzanine are gone but I hear voices above me from the loft. I look for signs of permanence, what is retained though long past. I walk out from the kitchen into the old side. It is in a state of disarray. Mary is there. She is going to reopen Somethyme. Everything will be the same. I ask: How can that be? Where will we find another barn? Suddenly I am confused. I think I might remember this actually happening, after Seventh Street had closed. Did it, or is this happening now? Mary asks if my check has cleared. I realize that either I don't remember anything OR that I no longer know the difference between the present and the past.

A dream about Mary: She and I are in the kitchen. She is telling me that a study showed that, if a business has just $900 in the bank they could make it. As she is telling me this, I am trying to put away a lot of plastic containers. They are stored on a ledge above the sinks. Each stack, a different size.

A dream about Elmer: I am in some kitchen, not my own, toasting my bread and pouring my coffee into a mug when someone says "Elmer is here." I go out and find an Elmer who has aged some but not to his current over-80 years. He is taller than I remembered. I said so. In response he kinda slouches down, leaning on a sideboard. I give him a hug, he kisses both my eyes. He said he has some old papers about the restaurant to show me, but they are so faded I can't read them.

The 30th Somethyme Reunion, October 2003

In 2003 we had a Somethyme 30th year reunion. This was the brainchild of Robin Moran and Jennie Knoop, who then enlisted the support of Bev Dawson, myself, and later Billy Stevens. We began getting together to make our plans, first at Anotherthyme to confer with Mary, but later mostly at Robin's house. We made a list of everyone we could remember who worked there, or were artists and musicians, or regular customers. We found out that 1104 Broad was unoccupied at the time as was the Under the Street space. 1102 had a restaurant in it and they were happy to have the extra business that this reunion would send their way. We could not have asked for a more perfect setting for the reunion.

We planned a quiet folkish/poetry night for Friday and dance music night with several bands playing for Saturday. We assembled refreshments and contracted with the owners of the building who had offered to provide a bar. We sold tickets to cover the expenses. We made sure that Elmer could be there. We invited people to bring memorabilia and offered a time for speakers to share memories. Mary took dinner reservations at Anotherthyme for a special night of Somethyme-themed meals.

We created buttons as souvenirs.

- Bet you can't remember my sign
- Young Republicans need not apply
- I can't believe I slept with you
- I can't believe I didn't sleep with you
- A woman needs a man like a fish needs a bicycle
- Another Stud for Peace
- Vegetarian and Proud
- I've forgotten everything I knew about living outside the

money economy
- Remind me who I was
- Five career changes later
- What would MSB do?
- I conquered Heather Mountain

We sent out emails, post cards, made phone calls with the pitch:

Greetings! Mary Rocap, Robin Moran, Jennie Knoop, Bev Dawson, and Billy Stevens, with help from Mary Bacon, have been meeting this summer to plan a 30th reunion celebration of the opening of Somethyme. We've been compiling the names of those that staffed the place, played music, hung their art on the walls, or were important to the community as customers, neighbors, and supporters. It's a long list of distinguished people and you are one of them. We hope you will come   the more the merrier! We're interested in seeing each of you and hearing your story.

In some ways our plans fell apart, but in other ways the reunion completely exceeded our expectations. More than 200 people came. Some from faraway places: New York City, Washington DC, Florida, California, Alaska even. We heard from many who could not make the trip. It was a wonderful time; all the faces were beautiful. People had gone on to lead accomplished lives. We looked at pictures of children we had never met. The space was familiar, but different; we were familiar, but different. There was a bond, you could feel it and know it to be true.

It was poignant to hear Robin speak of the openness that had existed at Somethyme. It was the last time I heard Brother Yusuf play; he was advanced in years and in ill health, but still radiating peace and love. Lise and I sang "O Freedom" to a hushed audience. Smiles and hugs and recollections of the goodness of the place and time abounded.

Robin Moran, Mary, Elmer, myself, Martha Maiden; October 2003

Bev Dawson, Linda Guthrie, Jeff Carter, Leslie Carter, Marilyn Roaf, Russ Rose;
October 2003

Happy Anniversary 2019

I have, over the years, posted something on Facebook on Somethyme's anniversary. The one I posted in 2019, for the 46th birthday, felt particularly meaningful. 83 responses with 147 comments. It was that posting that started me down this trek through memory. Here are some of those comments:

SomeThyme Restaurant opened on this day in 1973. 1104 Broad Street Durham. A shout out to all of you in the world that remember and blessings on you.

Jeff Carter *(staff and now a restaurateur himself!)*
My sentiments, as well. It was truly one big family.

Steven Petrow *(staff)*
Mary, Did you know that my first job was at SomeThyme? Yes. I did late night clean-up, which included mopping up the bathrooms. I learned so much from the graffiti in the women's bathroom. And I listened to and fell in love with Laura Nyro.

Erica Eisdorfer *(staff)*
I remember someone wrote "ytilaer si tahw" on the bathroom wall so when you were looking in the mirror, it read exactly correctly. I used to love that. Five years of waiting tables.

William Ben Spiller *(customer)*
All we ever did was eat there. With very young children. They had a wonderful sandwich for kids with honey and peanut butter and something else. What a wonderful memory of times as they once were.

Steven Ray Miller (staff and artist)

Grateful to have been paid 50 cents more per hour as a dishwasher. A bonus for "lack of human interaction." Ahh... the 70's!

Nancy Rosebaugh (customer)

I lived a block away from Somethyme in 1975 when I moved to Durham. One of my first outings was to a Triangle Friends of UFW benefit there where I met my dear friend Joan Preiss. Many delightful meals. Favorite food: MSB

Ann Bowman Alexander (customer and Wellspring founder)

Ate there every day for lunch for 3 months while opening Wellspring winter of 1981...many good friends worked there including you!!!

Anne Carter (staff)

Ann Alexander, I remember those days and those lunches. I couldn't conceive of what was going on there on 9th St. and what you and Portia and Flo were up to, but I knew it was big. Wellspring felt like a continuation of the love and values and communication of that love, those values, through food and hospitality that I had found at Somethyme. Home and home again. I am grateful for having been a part of these communities/alternative families, which definitely included our customers.

Libbie Hall (staff)

My 1st job fresh out of UNC CH with my English lit degree and love of cooking. 3 of the most educational and illuminating best years of my life. I learned from EVERYONE, and connected w so many great people. Janet Diamond taught me cooking, Mary Rocap taught me baking. The rainbow cast of out queer people expanded my work. So many crazy fun times and hard work and some heartbreak. Portia McKnight, Flo Hawley, Linda Guthrie, Marilyn Roaf, Anne Carter and siblings, Wicca Davidson, Laura (s), Leslie Tobin, MICKEY SAMUELS (biggest crush), Erica Eisdorfer, Helen Hancock, Kathy P, David, Gary. . . and so many more! Favorite food was not on the menu per se but I KNOW that Portia, Flo, Don and I made the best

Hashed Browns Mornay on Sunday mornings! My beloved late parents also loved Somethyme and I love memories of them dining there. And, of course, my legendary sister, Edna, known then as Mustang Edna. Somethyme forever.

Pattie Le Sueur (musician)

Somethyme was one of my favorite vegetarian restaurants. They had an incredible bean burger and I have not found its equal since. Our group, Triangle, played there about once a month or so. I still have some flyers. David McKnight on the fiddle and Jack LeSueur on guitar. Oh! And a free meal!

Billy Stevens (staff, musician)

I remember sitting at a booth with Mary, Elmer, Mary and Aden when Nona "sold" The Bluebird Cafe to become Somethyme. Worked there, played music there, hosted my parents on Graduation Weekend, too many memories beyond counting. Part of the inspiration for the Sallam, too. Thanks for the reminder, Mary.

Wicca Davidson (staff)

Never forgotten and always loved. SomeThyme was a huge part of my life and made me who I am. Early morning soup cooking, late night short order cook with Eben.

Sharon Snider Ringwalt (customer)

We loved eating there. Miss it still.

Bruce Piephoff (musician)

Played there many times in the 70s.

Kathryn Meyers (*friend, customer*)

I had dinner at Somethyme the nights both of my babies were born – 1975 and 1978. Great memories!

David Charles Terry (*Anotherthymer*)

Oh, I've heard plenty about those early days at Somethyme. It seems everyone who was interesting and a bit older than I was/am worked at Somethyme (or 9th Street Bakery) before I came onto the Anotherthyme scene in 1996 or so.

Anne Carter (*staff*)

I taught Mackey three vital knife-related lessons: 1) Never cut a cut (gesturing to a finger on my left hand) because that's what really hurts. 2) You'd think lemon hurts the most when it gets on your cut, but no, it's avocado, so try not to get that on there. But you will. 3) You're going to cut your cut again. You just will.

Useless advice to a new short order, stove cook, or third cook, yes, but surely words to live by. My heart is bursting with love for my Somethyme peeps and The Restaurant itself. So many, many great memories just from reading your list of names.

Jaki Shelton Green (*customer and Piedmont Poet Laureate*)

A favorite!

Jill Hofler (*customer*)

I remember it well. MSBs and red zinger tea.

Diane Pahl (*Knox Streeter*)

I remember sitting around the dining room table at Knox Street having a lively discussion of the possible names for the new establishment.

Susan Dunn *(Knox Streeter)*

I was there, painting the bathrooms, I believe. What a fine place!

Ninna Burkill *(customer)*

One of our favorite restaurants when we moved here in 1977. First restaurant where we had an entire meal with Peter sitting in a booster seat. Sweet memories.

Bob Goldman *(Knox Streeter)*

Wow!! So many fine people in one place, at one time, in a mutual configuration of spirit. Thanks Mary R. for starting this thread, thank you all for the reminders of a previous, happy life.

Who Worked There?
Both Somethyme and Seventh Street

(This is not an exhaustive list as it is based my memory and incomplete records. I do apologize if I left your name off.)

Somethyme interviews for front and kitchen staff every Monday, 10:30 – 1:00. We look for people who enjoy the ebb and flow of restaurant work and can bring something of themselves to the job. We ask for a 5-month commitment and a willingness to work at least 21 hours/week. We pool tips, have an in-house co-op, and health insurance benefits.

The Spectator classifieds, 11/9/1983

Geb Adams	Jane Adams	Aida ?
Mike Ancel	David Anderson	Monty Anderson
Ann Marie ?	David Bacon	Mary Bacon
Rodney Bass	David Beaudin	Jocelyn Berry
Chrissa Bertels	Marta Maria	Bruce Blevins
	Victoria Biette	
Bobby ?	Katherine Boquist	Greg Brown
Doug Broyles	Laura Byrant	Lawrence Bullock
Lavender Burris	Ann Bushyhead	Randy Campbell
Tom Campbell	Mackie Carroll	Anne Carter
Jeff Carter	Leslie Carter	Suzanne Casha
Ashley Chandler	Michael Chandler	Jeannie Cheeseman
Bonnie Cohen	Jane Collins	Jill Cotter
Steve Couch	Carole Cranor	cyn croxton
Paula Craig	Salinda Dahl	Cameron Dancy
Steve Darling	Al Dawson	Bev Dawson
Rick Darnell	Dennis DeJianne	Janet Diamond
Nancy Dickinson	Honorah Domizio	Helen Earle
Charlie Ebel	Erica Eisdorfer	Mary Ellis

Wendy Farrell Suzy Faulkner Valerie Faulkner
Keith Feather Jay Felton Aden Field
Anita Finch Laura Fortini Judy Frank
Jay Franklin Ron Franklin Sharon Funderburk
Billy Gaither Jeannie Gamble Tom Gatewood
Mike Geusz Jeanne Glasson Mara Gleason
Alice Glenn Diane Gore Garth Greene
Lydia Graham Mary Margaret Angie Greer
  Graham

Helen Griffin Jill Grossholz Linda Guthrie
Monica Halabas Edna Hall Elmer Hall
Libbie Hall Carl Hammond Chris Hammond
Michael Hammond Helen Hancock Martha Hankin
Leslie Hankins Jim Harb Rebecca Harvin
John Havran Flo Hawley David Hewett
Laura Hickok Lynn Hicks Ellen Hill
Dave Hirschman Hillary Honig Stu Hubbs
Robert Hulls Maclyn Humphries Rochelle Hunt
Apurba Islam Dorothy Jackson Barry Jacobs
John Jaffe Lynne Jaffe Jim Johnson
Amelia Jones Marjolein Kars Linda King
Jennie Knoop Ann Koons Randall Lanier
Larry ? Tristin Laughter Buddy Lemoine
Christie Lentz Susan Levy Joe Linus
Garry Lipscomb Jeanne Locher Doug Lowe
Dee Lutz Kendy Madden Rick Madden
Martha Maiden Biff Maier Nimes Mangum
Chris Mankoff Vinny Marra Peter Marsh
Jeff Marterer Pat Marterer Allen Mason
Joe Mattiacci Martha Mazonson Helga McAller
Robert McIlwee Libby McKeithen Portia McKnight
Pat McNellis Lisa Menafee Julie Menapace
Sandy Mercaldei Nancy Middleton Ann Miller

Meg Miller

Sofia Mohammed

Steve Mooney

Luna Mountainsea

Nate ?

Keith Nye

Stu Parrish

Sherry Paylor

Kathy Palletta

Jose Perara

Kent Phelps

Tom Prince

Eben Rawls

Maggie Rine

Molloy Rodgers

Lao Rubert

Maggie Schneider

Lila Shaara

John Soady

Dave Steere

Rob Sutter

Joe Thomas

Lise Uyanik

Julie Van Leuven

Lucy Wagner

Jenny Wears

Nancy Wharton

Michael Yellin

Steve Miller

Mo Mooney

Robin Moran

Michael Muller

Anne Newman

Elizabeth Oats

Patrick

David Payton

Shane Pennington

Steven Petrow

Andrew Preiss

Marsha Proctor

Sarah Reichman

Marilyn Roaf

Stacy Rose

Mickey Samuels

Brad Scott

Frank Shaw

Sheryl Soady

Billy Stevens

Randy Talley

Leslie Tobin

Carlton Van Court

Nancy Vest

Cory Walker

Stacy Weaver

Margo Williams

Ruth Ziegler

Michael Mitchel

Michael Mooney

Jonathan Moss

Annie Nashold

Eduardo Nunez

Bo Osborne

Wicca Paull

David Palletta

Eileen Penot

Stephano Petrucci

Rachel Preston

Lanier Rand

Russel Rigsbee

Mary Rocap

Sherri Rosenthal

Tony Scheer

Lorisa Seibel

Tim Smith

Susan Soltis

Suzanne Sturm

Steve Tapp

Don Underhill

Erica Van Court

Sara Via

Doug Watson

Susan Wetzler

John Wilson

People I Fired

Michael for continuing to add cayenne to the fried potatoes.

John for having a lit pipe of pot in his coat pocket which was hanging in the back hallway.

And, oh my goodness, so many dishwashers who didn't show up.

Some Memories from Folks Who Remember Making Me Mad

I may have had the honor of being one of the few people to make Mary Rocap furiously angry. I came home late one night and had a message to go make the tuna salad for the street fair happening the next day. Another staff member was with me and we were both slightly tipsy. We went to the restaurant, and I called out the ingredients and she brought them to me. Somehow paprika and hot chili pepper got mixed up. The next day at the street fair, poor Mary had been selling tuna salad sandwiches, and having them returned as they were so so so hot. When I got there for my shift Mary Rocap gave me a look I will never forget.   -Wicca

And another:

I just remembered putting on Chris Williamson during my cashier shift and you coming out of the kitchen and turning it off. You had definitely heard it one too many times.   -Martha

Wicca Paull also remembers me doing this when she played the tape. I must really have heard it way too often.

In Memoriam

Sadly, there are those we love but see no longer. Part of our story died with them. Part of their story lives on in our memory. To these souls I know to have passed on: Bonnie Cohen, Suzy Faulkner, Aden Field, Billy Gaither, Jennie Knoop, Jeanne Locklear, Nimes Mangum, Sue Sneddon, Carlton van Court, Erica van Court, Gary Wein, Nancy Wharton – May you have found rest from your labors.

Vendors and Products

CLEANING PRODUCTS

Mary was responsible for the type of cleaning supplies we used. Her sister Susan was a Shaklee distributor and we used the product Basic H as a cleaner. Developed in the 1960s, Basic-H was one of the first environmentally safe household cleaners on the market. It claims to be the world's most versatile cleaner and was named an official Earth Day product. We also used Dr. Bronner's Peppermint Castile Soap. The soap is great but the labels are fantastic. They are chock-full of his philosophy, which he called "All-One-God-Faith" and many statements such as: "We're all sisters & brothers!" and "Have courage and smile, my friend. Think and act 10 years ahead!" and "Balanced food for body – mind – soul – spirit is our medicine!" and "Breathe deeply!"

BIGGERS BROTHERS

Biggers Brothers was our conventional wholesale distributor. This was another major order to make and to put away. Lots of number 10 cans of tomatoes (whole, puree, crushed) and the more common items we stocked the kitchen with.

Here is a sample order:
- 1 vanilla (1 quart)
- 2 trash bags (100 count/box)
- 2 mayo (4 gallon jars/case)
- 1 red wine vinegar (4 gallon jars/case)
- 1 light syrup (4 gallon jars/case)
- 1 artichoke hearts (6 #10 cans/case)
- 1 tuna (6 66½ oz cans/case)

- 1 butter chips (4 200-count boxes/case)
- 1 almond extract (1 quart)
- 5 whole tomatoes (6 #10 cans/case)
- 1 crushed tomatoes (6 #10 cans/case)
- 1 tomato puree (6 #10 cans/case)
- 1 equal (1,000 packets/case)
- 1 sugar in the raw (1,000 packets/case)
- 1 cranberry cocktail (12 46-oz cans/case)
- 1 tomato juice (12 46-oz cans/case)
- 1 frozen spinach (12 3# boxes/case)
- 1 frozen shrimp (12 5# boxes/case)

BRAME SPECIALTY COMPANY

We got our paper products from Brame: paper towels, napkins, to-go containers, order pads. During the '70s a sales representative would stop by the restaurant weekly, even if we didn't order something every time he came. There was a gentility to this system that I miss in these days of online ordering or talking to a machine.

CLARK'S SEAFOOD

The husband and wife seafood operation of the Clarks, on Morehead Street, was our link to the coast. They would drive to Morehead City once or twice a week to pick up fresh fish and shrimp. They would shell the shrimp or sell it unshelled; you could get the fish whole or filleted. They didn't deliver, but since it was close, it was easy enough for one of us to pick it up in the way in.

CORNUCOPIA

Food distributor Cornucopia Cheese & Specialty Foods Company was founded in 1980 in the back room of a community grocery store in nearby Alamance County. We got our feta, olives, parmesan, and other specialty items from them.

GREEN MOUNTAIN HERBS

The spice closet was in the back of the back of the kitchen, around the corner from the walk-in, a semi-private place where you could have a semi-private conversation. The walls in that area still had the pumpkin orange that we painted it prior to our opening. The health department allowed us to keep it on the walls since it was in a storage rather than production area.

My most vivid memory of the spices comes from a time when I was emptying the contents of a bag of cayenne pepper into a plastic air-tight container. After a bit of time I found that I had a nose bleed. The strength of the pepper that I breathed burned through my little capillaries. That's some fresh (and strong) cayenne.

KAPLAN RESTAURANT SUPPLIES

Sandy Kaplan was our favorite gadget guy. We bought china, glassware, and kitchen tools, from spatulas to slicers, from him. I still have some glasses from the Arcoroc line that are incredibly resistant to breakage. Over the years he became a friend. One year after Anotherthyme opened, Helen Griffin, former Somethymer and the then kitchen manager at Anotherthyme, and I went up to a restaurant supply show in DC that Kaplan Supplies was putting on. We felt very entrepreneur-ish and cosmopolitan, staying in a hotel, and buying things we thought we needed.

KUTTER'S CHEESE

Kutter's Cheese is a traditional cheese factory located in Corfu, New York. Begun in 1923 by the German immigrant Leo Kutter, it has continued as a family business, now in its third generation of leadership. Every three weeks they would send a truck down, always with the same hale and hearty driver who was usually wearing a red plaid flannel shirt. We ordered NY sharp cheddar, mild cheddar, and whole milk mozzarella. Their mild cheddar is still my favorite cheddar flavor, though I haven't had any since Somethyme.

LATTA EGGS

Latta Eggs came from Hillsborough, and they were another family business. We generally ordered 90 dozen eggs a week, a heavy week would be 120 dozen. Mostly they delivered, but sometimes we picked them up. They had a small shed on Pickett Road where they stored eggs for such occasions. Unrefrigerated. Unlocked. No one there. They were trusting souls. They began their business just after WWII ended and are still at it. According to their website, their hens produce 30,000 eggs a day.

LINDLEY MILLS

Lindley Mills, Inc. is a 10th generation organic specialty flour mill and mix manufacturer located in Graham, North Carolina. It began in 1755. Orange County was established in 1752 so that makes them a very early-on-the-scene business. Joe Lindley, the current president of the company, proudly says, "There was a Lindley's Mill before there was a United States of America."

The family lost control of the mill in 1855 but got it back in 1975. Since then, they have milled exclusively organic grains. We got a weekly delivery. Their delivery person was a very friendly and gentle African American man. When I started baking for the Chapel Hill Farmer's Market in 2009 I ordered my flour from them. I found that, even though thirty-some years had gone by, I still knew their phone number by heart. Since they would not deliver the smaller quantities that I now ordered, I would make the trip out to their mill in Graham (on the road that bears their name) to pick up the flour. One day I saw a tall, lean African American man that looked just like our former delivery person. I went over to him and found that he was that man's son.

LONG MEADOW DAIRY

We got our dairy products from Long Meadow, a local dairy. This was the easiest vendor to order from since the delivery person walked in, assessed our needs, brought the product in, and stocked it. That was service. We had the same delivery person for years and years.

A SOUTHERN SEASON

One of my favorite procurement trips was to A Southern Season. During the later days of the restaurant, on my "day off" I would go shopping for the place. First, I would go to Thomas & Howard in Durham, a retail-style wholesaler and then head off to Chapel Hill for smoked bluefish, items from The Silver Wok, and finally to A Southern Season. Here I would pick up freshly roasted coffee and Callebaut chocolate; the smell in my car from those items made the return trip so worth it.

SYKES ICE HOUSE

There was an ice house downtown on Roxboro Road (I think it was Sykes) that made ice in quantity. Picking up our daily supply was Elmer's job mostly. We sure were happy the day we got our own ice machine installed.

TREE OF LIFE

We ordered weekly from Tree of Life. At the time, they were the largest wholesale natural food distributor around. They drove their big wheeler from St. Augustine, Florida to park along Broad Street, taking up many parking spaces, hopefully before we opened. We got our organic beans, grains, turbinado sugar, and oils from them. They also brought us our organic carrots. Putting away that order was an all-hands-on-deck operation. Most of that stuff went on the mezzanine. Even I could get a 50-pound bag up there, lifting it up step-by-step, not carrying it, just moving it along one step at a time.

WARD'S FRUIT & PRODUCE

Our produce came from Ward's. They were a family-run business and were headed, back then, by Bebe and her father Howard. Although their roots were in Durham, they had moved to the grounds of the Raleigh Farmers Market. We had to place our order by 5:00 the afternoon before the delivery, but if you forgot something you could wake up real early to call them, and they were usually able to tack it onto the order.

KITCHEN TOOLS

To this day, the knives that I think of as essential are the ones I learned to use at the restaurant. Foremost, the Caddie Knife. This is a Japanese vegetable chopping knife that was most often in my hand as I worked. Although we had knife racks which held knives anyone could use during a shift, it was a good to have your own. Sharpening the knives on a whetstone with oil was usually the first thing you did when you started a shift. Everyone's angle is a little different so you wanted a knife that stayed yours. We bought them from Tree of Life and cooks could order their own at the wholesale cost.

My next favorite was a tomato knife, a small serrated knife, perfect for tomatoes and citrus.

A sharp bread knife was needed for slicing all that bread but also for slicing mozzarella. Aden Field was the best mozzarella slicer we had.

Some People

Really, everyone has a story. But I'll have to let these few suffice.

David Beaudin

David was a consummate wait person. Always professional. Always considerate. He was on the Personal Committee, I believe the longest of anyone. He kept being willing to run and he kept being elected. In truth, he is an artist. He ended up working at the NC Museum of Art as a master framer with a specialty in gilding.

Lawrence Bullock

Lawrence grew up in Durham and began working at Somethyme maybe when he was still in high school. Even at that age, it was obvious that he was full of talent. He was a poet and confident enough to give readings; he was a musician and confident enough to perform. He moved to California and became an actor and playwright.

Randy Campbell

Probably the kindest wait staff person that ever was. After the restaurant, he worked many years at the Regulator Bookshop. When we moved to Hillsborough and started going to St. Matthew's Episcopal Church, I was happy to see that he and his husband, Steven Burke, were members. He and Steven have the most amazing collection of tiny folk art buildings, over 1,200, possibly the largest in the world, all displayed or stored in their home "It Had Wings" (named after Allan Gurganus' short story of the same name). Their collection is one of the crown jewels of Hillsborough.

BEV DAWSON

Bev; photo by Martha Maiden, 1975

I believe Bev and Al were already a couple when they began working at Somethyme. Al was a bar person and Bev a wait and cook. Bev and I have the same birthday. Bev was great at everything she did. She was also a seamstress and made my first wedding dress and the dress I wore for my sister's wedding. Bev also made most, if not all, of the tablecloths and aprons for the front staff. Now that I think of it that may have put me in the mind to make aprons as one of the things I could sell at the farmer's market. At the time there were still lots of fabric outlets along Hwy 85 heading towards Burlington. We would go and select the fabric and buy a couple of bolts. Aprons were generally denim, forest green, or dark brown color. The tablecloths varied. We had a checked pattern of various colors, but my favorite fabric was a deep red one with hints of other colors in the thread; it was a heavy, loose weave and laid well across the tables. The two of us considered opening up a bakery together, but we didn't. Bev and I were also canning partners. We used the sterilizer sink to water-bath peaches. Later, she became a Bradley Method Birthing Teacher, and Tom and I took her class in preparation for our daughter Marielle's birth. Al is a musician and although we never played together, we have many mutual friend bandmates.

Bev taught me how to assemble a grilled cheese sandwich. I know you are thinking, there is a way? Yes, there is. Cut your bread, butter one of the slices and place it on your work surface so that the buttered side is facing up. Butter the other slice and place it butter side down on top of the other slice. The buttered slices are now facing each other. Add your sliced cheese. Then, take your stack to the grill, griddle, or heated pan, place the portion of the sandwich from the slice with the cheese on top and lay it on the heated surface (the buttered side will be facing down) then take the remaining buttered bread and place it on top (the buttered side facing up). If you do it this way, your fingers won't ever be smeared with butter. To this day, I always use Bev's technique.

ERICA EISDORFER

Erica is someone who would continue to have an impact on my life. She spent years managing the Bull's Head Bookshop, the bookstore for the UNC Chapel Hill campus. My girls worked there as students, both Marielle and Christiana. She is now at Flyleaf Books. I'm proud to have this intergenerational relationship with her.

ADEN FIELD

Aden was a friend of Knox Street and the first person we hired for the kitchen staff; he was critically important to the beginning of the restaurant. In addition to being an accountant, he was a poet, author, playwright, and cook. He began working with the three of us even before the restaurant opened. Once we opened, he became the main short-order cook and soup-maker. Aden became a close friend – one year even spending the Christmas holiday with my family in Pennsylvania, where he endeared himself to everyone by reciting *The Night Before Christmas* from memory, with poetic and dramatic flair, on Christmas Eve.

He was born in 1938 in McKenzie, Tennessee. Following his graduation from Harvard, he came to Durham to go to graduate school at Duke. Though he didn't finish his degree, he didn't leave town. Aden liked to create structure. He did that from an accountant's perspective and from an organizer's perspective. After three years at Somethyme, he left to open The Regulator Bookshop with Tom Campbell (another Somethymer). Somethyme was a better place because Aden was there. When he left, we wished him and Tom well; there were no hard feelings. I made the first curtains for the Regulator's windows.

He stayed at the Regulator until 1978. At some point he also opened up his own (short-lived) restaurant, on the second floor above The Ivy Room. It was named after his mother: Eddie's. He continued to do accountant work throughout the rest of his life for Durham non-profits.

His papers are archived at Duke's Library. From the website: "This collection consists of his journals, writings, postcard collections, community projects and files, and his collection of correspondence and writings from friends and family. It documents his friendships and relationships, Durham community events and activities, and his career as a writer and teacher in North Carolina."

Aden making MSBs; photo by Jonathan Moss, 1974

LIBBIE AND EDNA HALL

These sisters, born in Durham, are another of what I call our Dynasties. We were honored to know their whole family because their parents were faithful customers. Libby would go on to be a prime employee at Ninth Street Bakery and Edna became an educator. They were positive in outlook but able to convey truth when truth was needed. I always trusted them.

JIM HARB

I always experienced Jim as a joyful human being who delighted in the small things: marinated red onions, for example. He was, like many of our staff, vastly over-qualified as a short-order cook with his sharp, inquisitive, and expansive mind. He was always ready to go deep in any conversation.

LAURA HICKOK

Laura's birthday is the day before mine. We often went to the Driver's License Bureau together to renew our driver's licenses, which had to be renewed every year and required passing a written test. Laura became a trusted friend to both myself and Tom. She was the first person we ever let babysit Marielle. She also kept Marielle overnight when we went to the hospital to deliver Christiana. One of my favorite Thanksgiving memories is being invited to share the holiday with her parents in Winston-Salem. Her mother served baked brussel sprouts with grated parmesan cheese on top. It was the first time I ever had eaten them and they were delicious. After dinner we went into the den and watched the entire *Tinker Tailor Soldier Spy* series with superb cups of coffee to keep us awake.

Portia McKnight & Flo Hawley

Portia was a wait person and a short-order cook. She never wore a dress. I think several of the guys on staff took to kidding her about that and said if she ever wore a dress to work, they would wear one too. Well, she came into work one day wearing a dress and the next day, those guys did too. One was waiting tables and one was cooking. That happened to be a day my parents were in town visiting. It may have even been a super busy day, like a holiday, like Easter. It was funny, it was embarrassing, and it was just like us being flippant and testy, casual and argumentative, all at the same time.

Flo was a stalwart baker who, along with Portia, left us for Wellspring when they opened. Both Portia and Flo left the retail world in 2000 to open a cheese-making business, Chapel Hill Creamery. They hired Marielle as a cheese-maker the summer before her senior year in high school. She continued to work there during her college years at UNC/Chapel Hill. Marielle is a poet and gifted them with a poem upon leaving that job. Every Christmas holiday they make a special package for their Carolina Moon cheese and include a copy of that poem within the box. (Thank you for that!)

Little Known Fact: Portia, Flo, and David Beaudin all wear the same size shoe.

STEVE MILLER

Steven Ray Miller was a very early member of the staff and community of Somethyme. Mostly he was known for postcard versions of his artwork which he sold at the cashier station for 25 cents apiece on the honor system. I am a postcard enthusiast and bought quite a few myself. His iconic painting of Bev Dawson and Nancy Dickinson standing in front of the restaurant graces the cover of this book. I own a copy of the print and have had it since I bought it at a show of his that Somethyme hosted. Now it hangs in my home and I look at it every day.

ROBIN MORAN

Robin was a Duke alumni making her living as a carpenter. One of my favorite social memories of that era is that for several years a bunch of us Somethymers would go to Mary Bacon's house to watch the World Series. 1980 was memorable because we, as a group, were Phillies fans and they won that year. We were fans, in part, because their star pitcher, Steve Carlton, was a relative of Robin's, a cousin maybe.

EDUARDO NUNEZ

Eduardo was one of the few of what I would call professional waits we had at the restaurant. He and his friend, José Perara. Eduardo had worked, or was working at the same time, at Bakatsias, the first of restaurateur Giorgios Bakatsias' many places. Eduardo came to work in a black suit, white shirt, and tie. He was famously cordial and raised the level of service in our humble establishment simply with his presence. At the time of Seventh Street, he and his wife had opened a little fresh pasta business called Que Pasta. We would commission special pastas to go with our pasta specials. The one that I remember the most vividly was a lemon-pepper linguini.

RACHEL PRESTON

Rachel was an alumni of both Duke and of Omega House (Year Three). It was through this association that I first met her. Rachel was a crafter. Her parents, Don & Sue Preston, had a family macramé side business of which Rachel was a part. They were regular craft market vendors who sold up and down the East Coast, including the prestigious Carolina Friends School's annual Easter Craft Fair. Rachel and I considered opening a bakery together but only got as far as getting a NC tax ID number for sales tax. When Tom moved to Durham in 1981, he and Rachel were housemates at Monkeytop (another Durham counter-culture institution along with its neighbor mansion Sunnyside). After Somethyme, she started a landscaping business and hired Tom. At Somethyme, Rachel was a baker, and whenever we had staff meetings she would bring some handwork to keep her fingers busy as we sat in a circle and talked. She made potholders using the Cathedral Windows pattern. I followed her example and began to make my own potholders, many years later, selling them first at the Hillsborough Farmers Market and then at the Chapel Hill Farmers Market. But I don't make that Cathedral Windows pattern; that pattern is much too precise.

RUSSELL RIGSBEE

Russell is a well-regarded and well-known photographer and stained glass artist who lived nearby. His family goes back generations in Durham. It was Rigsbee family land in Pinhook that Erwin Mills purchased for their enterprise. Russell worked as a busser for a while, but was mostly a beloved customer. He would sit in a two-top in the back, and if you weren't busy he was always game for a chat. His wife Peaches had a typesetting and printing business and produced many of our menus. Russell was paid a bottomless cup of coffee for some of the things he made Somethyme. Tom tells me that Russell went to the doctor about heart palpitations and his doctor asked him how much coffee he was drinking. Upon hearing about eight cups a day, the doctor advised him to consider cutting back some.

SUZANNE STURM

Me and Suzanne; photo by Tom, 1986

Hard worker with a heart of gold. A friend to both me and Tom. A ceramic artist, a talent that she passed down to her grandson. A couple of my favorite pieces of art that we own are hers: a foot-high, painted, Papier-mâché rocking chair and two ceramic mythical horse-somethings, all completely fanciful. I consider our working relationship to be the best I ever had. As this picture suggests, we always had each other's back.

NANCY WHARTON

Nancy brought her fiercely loyal spirit to the hard work of keeping the place clean. She held down both dishwashing and clean-up shifts. She also worked at the Duke Lemur Center. Once she brought a lemur to the restaurant in her shirt pocket; its long fingers extending from inside and its big eyes peeking out from above the pocket line. That is one of my all-time favorite memories.

Recipes

Our recipes cards generally only gave the list of ingredients, not details about their assemblage or cooking instructions. I've added a few notes, but not much in the way of instructions. Neither have I reduced the ingredient quantities for home style versions.

Oatmeal Bread

Proof:

    4 cups milk, scalded

    1 ½ cup warm water

    1 ½ cup molasses

    2 T. yeast

Sponge: In which you add all the measured ingredients, with the exception of salt, and whisk. Continue to whisk, as you add flour, until it is the consistency of a thick pancake batter.

    ½ cup oil

    5 cups oats

    2 cups unbleached flour

Finishing up:

    1 T. salt

    Whole wheat flour to finish

Summer Sandwich (used with the oatmeal bread)

    Cream cheese

    Home grown tomato slices

    Black Pepper

    Cucumber slices

    Avocado

    Spike

    Shredded Lettuce

SEVENTH STREET'S MIXED GRAIN BREAD

Proof:

> 1 ½ cup molasses
>
> 9 cups water
>
> 3 T. yeast

Sponge:

> 4 ½ cups oatmeal
>
> 1 ½ cups yellow corn meal
>
> ¾ cup bran
>
> 3 cups unbleached flour
>
> ¾ cup oil

Finishing Up:

> 1 T. salt
>
> Whole wheat flour for the remainder

TOMATO-BASIL BREAD

Proof:

> Heated 46-oz jar of tomato juice
>
> 2 T. sugar
>
> 2 T. yeast

Sponge:

> 1 egg
>
> ½ cup oil
>
> 2 T. basil

Finishing Up:

> 1 T. salt
>
> Unbleached flour for the remainder

DRESSING FOR MARINATED MOZZARELLA

1 cup + 2 T. extra virgin olive oil
1 cup soy oil
1 ¼ t. red pepper flakes
5 T. minced parsley
2 T. minced basil (fresh) or 2 t. dry
2 T. minced green onion tops
1 ¼ t. minced garlic

POMODORO BASILICA SANDWICH (on Tomato-Basil Bread)

Marinated Mozzarella (see above)
sliced tomato
¼ avocado
grilled mushrooms (with garlic salt)
basil pesto mayonnaise (mayonnaise with some pesto stirred in)
lettuce

PYEWACKET'S (FAILED!) HONEY-WHEAT BERRY BREAD

Pressure Cook 1 cup dry wheat berries until done
Proof:
1 2/3 cup dry milk
5 ½ water
1 cup honey
2 T. yeast
Sponge:
½ cup oil
½ cup wheat germ
½ cup bran
Added cooked wheat berries

Finishing Up:
   1T. salt
   Whole wheat flour for the remainder

DILL BREAD (used for the egg salad and chicken salad sandwiches)

Proof:
   4 cups milk, warmed
   1 cup warm water
   ½ cup sugar
   2 T. yeast

Sponge:
   2 eggs
   2 T. minced onion
   1 ½ T. dill weed
   ½ cup sour cream
   ½ cup oil

Finishing Up:
   1 T. salt
   Unbleached flour for the remainder

MARY'S (ME-MARY) GINGER BREAD (based on *The Tassajara Bread Book* recipe)

Whisk:
   6 eggs
   4 cups molasses
   2 cups margarine (melted)

Sift:

    1 cup powdered milk

    9 cups whole wheat flour

    2 T. baking powder

    1 T. baking soda

    2 t. salt

    1 T, 2 t. cinnamon

    2 T. powdered ginger

    1 T., 1 t. dry mustard

    2 t. cloves

Mix the sifted ingredients with 4 cups hot water then add the whisked ingredients

Bake in 3 pans at 350 degrees for 20 minutes, don't overcook. After baking, pierce the cakes with fork before spreading sauce on cake. (Always make the sauce.)

Sauce:

    ¾ cup melted butter

    ¾ cup grated lemon peel

    3/8 cup honey

TWEED CAKE (from my mother: a frequent birthday special dinner request)

Cream:

    ½ cup butter

    1 cup sugar

    1 t. vanilla

Dry:

    2 cups sifted unbleached flour

    1 T. baking powder

    A pinch of salt

Wet:

    1 cup milk

    2 eggs

    Add wet and dry alternately to creamed mixture.

    Stir in 3 oz. grated unsweetened chocolate

    Fold in 3 beaten egg whites

Icing:

    ¾ cup butter

    3 egg yolks

    2 ¼ cup powdered sugar

Ice the cake, then melt 2 oz. semi-sweet chocolate in 3 T warm water and drizzle over the cake

APPLE CAKE (my Great-Aunt Clara's recipe)

Sift:

    3 cups unbleached flour

    1 T baking powder

    2 cups sugar

Mix:

    1 cup soy oil

    1/3 cup orange juice

    2 ½ t vanilla

    4 egg yolks

Add to dry ingredients

Beat 4 egg whites fill fluffy and fold into batter

Slice a small mixing bowl of apples thinly (4-5 apples)

Layer into a greased tube pan

½ batter, apples, sprinkled cinnamon, batter, apples, cinnamon

Bake at 350 degrees for at least one hour

BLUEBERRY STREUSEL PIE (makes 4)

Mix:

    16 cups blueberries (thaw if frozen)

    6 and 2/3s cups sour cream

    1 cup unbleached flour

    3 T. vanilla

    2 t. salt

    3 cups sugar

    4 eggs

Bake in 4 unbaked pie shells: 10 min. 450 degrees, 35 min. 350 degrees

Mix:

    3 cups chopped walnuts

    1 ½ cups unbleached flour

    3 sticks butter

    1 cup turbinado sugar

    1 cup light brown sugar

    1-2 T. molasses

    ¼ t. salt

    2 ½ T. cinnamon

Press onto tops of pies (cover completely) bake 15 more minutes at 350

SUGAR CHEESECAKES (6)

Crust:

    6 cups graham cracker crumbs

    1# melted margarine

    2 T. cinnamon

    ½ cup sugar

Bake crust at 300 degrees for 8 – 10 minutes

Filling:

    14 egg yolks

    4 T. vanilla

    4 T. flour

    2 t. ground ginger

    3 ½ cups sugar

Add: blend low

    3 big scoops cottage cheese (I don't remember what this measurement was; possibly 2 cups each)

    5 ½ # cream cheese

    1 pint whipping cream

    ¾ cup lemon juice

In a large, dry bow beat 10 egg whites and fold into filling

Pour into 6 pans and bake at 300 degrees for 40 minutes (rotate pans during baking and check for doneness at 30 minutes.

Topping:

    ½ container sour cream (4 cups)

    ½ cups sugar

    1 t. vanilla

Acknowledgements

Thank you to those who I talked with early on about their memories of the restaurant especially my husband, Tom Prince, former partners Martha Maiden and Lise Uyanik Ebel, former staffers, Barry Jacobs and Wicca Davidson, and long-time friend, performer, and customer Georgann Eubanks.

Thank you to those who read early versions of this work: Christiana Amis, Georgann Eubanks, Christine Hale, Martha Hankin LeFebvre, and Nancy Rosebaugh.

Thank you to Jacob Thomas for teaching me enough about Microsoft Word to format the book.

Thank you to Steven Ray Miller for allowing me to use his iconic painting "Bev and Nancy" for the cover of this book; to Martha Maiden for giving me permission to use the astrological birth chart she had created for me long ago and then for working one up for Somethyme; and once again to Georgann, for permission to include her poem "A Place To Come To" which was printed on the back of one of our menus.